MIDWEST FUTURES

MIDWEST FUTURES

Phil Christman

Belt Publishing

Portions of this book appeared in different form in the *Hedgehog Review.*

Printed in the United States of America

ISBN: 978-1-953368-08-9

Belt Publishing
5322 Fleet Avenue
Cleveland, OH 44105
www.beltpublishing.com

Book design by Meredith Pangrace
Cover by David Wilson

To Ashley, who asked

A NOTE ON THE TEXT

As the Midwest was surveyed into six-by-six square-mile grids, this book consists of six rows containing six prose "plats," each approximately 1,000 words long.

ROW 1

THE FUND

By the side of Ohio Route 38, about two miles past East Liverpool, you can visit the place where the Midwest does not begin.

What you can see at that spot is an unassuming little obelisk with a plaque on its front. One historian who traveled "several thousand miles" to find it still overshot it and had to turn around. On either side is just enough room for a few cars to pull off the road and park. You picture a Dad emerging from a station wagon. You hear him intoning, in that voice available only to Dads moved to reverence by historical markers, "Guys, come look at this," as the children blink. "Boy, isn't this something," he finally says, and someone sighs with relief, for he is almost done, and there is no bathroom. McDonald's was miles ago.

(Well—that is what I pictured, anyway, one summer afternoon in Ann Arbor, as I gazed at this spot on Google Maps, wondering if I should, like another generation's crusading *litterateur*, simply drive there. James Agee would drive there. But James Agee, burdened and guilty as he was, did not yet know about carbon footprints. Back to Google Maps it was, then, and my little reverie, a cultural memory of a summer-vacationing Middle American normality that I feel I should somehow claim, though it is not mine.)

So much for the little pointed rock that memorializes the place known to history as the Beginning Point of the U.S. Public Lands Survey.

Roughly 1,000 feet south of this monument, on Saturday, August 20, 1785, a surveyor crossed the Ohio River and placed a small stake in the ground. By doing so, this unknown surveyor—a member of the team tasked by the governments of Virginia and Pennsylvania with finding, or naming, or inventing the invisible lines that demarcate these states from each other—initiated the mapping of another series of boundaries: between the vast territory to the west and the thirteen states that it might enrich, between the new frontier and the old colonies it might render irrelevant. Mapping is, in its way, a form of creation. The next day, a Sunday, the team rested.

On September 30 of that year, a second team returned to that spot and headed west, measuring off the land in the English style, with sixty-six-foot lengths of chain. This team was led by Thomas Hutchins, recently appointed as official geographer to the provisionally United States of America, and he had orders from Congress—the Land Ordinances of 1784 and 1785. These Acts told the surveyors to map this wild place into townships: squares six miles per side, divided into thirty-six little square-mile boxes. "This was a revolutionary concept," writes historian Andro Linklater. "For centuries the land had been lived in by the Delaware and passed through by the Miami and occupied by the Iroquois, but no one had ever owned it." Owning and living upon are separate, indeed often opposed, things.

One architect of this project was Thomas Jefferson, whose 1784 *Report on Government for Western Territory* inspired both ordinances. In some of his many moods, he envisioned each square as an affordable home for a hardy yeoman farmer. (These moods, which Jefferson was capable of abandoning when necessary, constitute the thing historians call, with undue reverence, "Jeffersonian democracy.") He believed that the competition between small farms would generate a hardy, self-sufficient people, ready for self-government. To set this "natural" process in motion required prior central planning—Culture completing Nature, in the Enlightenment style.

Hutchins's notes on the land are enough to fire the imagination of any Jeffersonian democrat. "The land is remarkably rich," he later wrote to Congress, "with a deep black mould, free from stone . . . it is well adapted for indian [sic] corn, tobacco, hemp, flax, oats, etc, and every species of garden vegetables." He describes an agrarian utopia, square after square of mellow fruitfulness.

He also describes another people's land—a fact that should concern us, and that did, in another way, come to concern him. Soon after they began, Hutchins's team crossed paths with a second group, led by General Richard Butler, a Revolutionary War veteran who like many such veterans hoped to claim some long-overdue backpay in the form of Western plats of his own. He was on his way to purchase (that is, swindle) land from the Miami tribe, so that the western encroachment of the United States could continue. If Hutchins's letters to Congress conjure a small farmer's paradise, Butler in his journal reminds us what all this measuring and describing and scrutinizing led to, describing the survey team as "a set of gentlemen who are the first at work on a fund which will eventually . . . extinguish the debt of the United States." Not a place—a fund. Big Eastern land speculators already eyed these plats.

Funds, like states, require central authority and a monopoly on force. Otherwise you just have claims and counterclaims of credit and ownership, back and forth, forever. Butler notes in his journal, with some consternation, that Hutchins expected to have to quit soon, because most of the soldiers providing Hutchins's team with safe conduct would join Butler at the negotiations. Hutchins's team—their notes a riot of clashing methodologies—did indeed stop after a handful of miles, fearing Native attack. December found Hutchins in New York, rhapsodizing to Congress about Ohio dirt. Without military support, which a weak Confederation Congress could not yet provide, Ohio Territory could be some people's home, but precisely not "a fund."

So much for the spot that opened the way to the Midwest. So much, as well, for the little stone monument that memorializes but, as we've seen, doesn't actually mark it. The exact point about 1,000 feet south, from which Hutchins set out, is, according to some sources, somewhere on the property of FirstEnergy, whose permission the would-be visitor must request. Another source insists that it is beneath a loading dock owned by a logistics company, S.H. Bell. Still others say it is underwater.

How characteristic of the Midwest that its first spot should be like this: a pivot point in American history, permanently out of focus. This is the way the Midwest exists in the American mind: massively there, constantly eluding our grasp. "The Midwest," wrote Michael Martone, "is hard to see, especially when you are in it."

The word itself sounds self-contradictory: Mid/West. Which is it: middle, or western? According to the U.S. Census Bureau, "Midwest" names a region that either subsumes or includes bits of a number of other, distinct geographic or cultural regions—parts of Great Lakes Country (Michigan, Wisconsin, Minnesota, Ohio, Indiana, Illinois, but not, of course, Canada); parts of the Great Plains (Illinois, Iowa, Kansas, Nebraska, the Dakotas, but not Montana); parts of the Cotton and Rust Belts (but not Western Pennsylvania); even parts of the South (Missouri). It includes sections of the country that "belonged" to the U.S. at the time the Constitution was ratified—the so-called Old Northwest Territory, ceded from the British in the Treaty of Paris, that Hutchins and his team began to survey (it later became Ohio, Indiana, Illinois, and Michigan, plus parts of Wisconsin and Minnesota). It includes several states that took the right side of the Civil War and one (Missouri) that didn't quite make up its mind. (At one point Missouri's government, like the medieval papacy, had two competing claimants.) It also includes parts of the Louisiana Purchase. It cuts through the Ozarks and Black Hills, the Ozark and Appalachian Plateaus, some of the Missouri and Mississippi Rivers, and several major aquifers, but it does not encompass any of them; we cannot look to geography to give it coherence. The region is a conceptual magpie's nest, made from scraps of everything.

This assumes, of course, that you follow the definition of the U.S. Census Bureau. Almost nobody does. A recent survey found that 10 percent of respondents would consider Montana, Wyoming, Colorado, Pennsylvania, and West Virginia Midwestern; a somewhat higher percentage would throw in Kentucky and Oklahoma. Not a single state won a hundred percent of the vote, though Illinois came closest, with 81percent.

In addition to the non-Midwestern states people *think* are Midwestern—I, personally, am dovish on the question of Western Pennsylvanian inclusion—there are the Midwestern states folks refuse to recognize as such. Many people solemnly avow that Kansas and Nebraska are doing their own thing, that Indiana is a lost bit of the South. Some say that Michigan, my home, is just "the North." The U.S., of course, does not have a "North," any more than Detroit, *pace* the narrator of Journey's "Don't Stop Believin'," has a "South." Conceptually, we have a northeast, a northwest, and a *mid*west. If you're a Southerner, you may also recognize a category called "Yankees"; escaped slaves, Great Migrators, and midcentury Appalachians looking for work *headed* north. But there is no place that is just "The North."

Perhaps the term is simply colonial-geographical: you're in the western part of the United States, but, you know, you're kind of halfway through it. But this only works until you look at a map of the forty-eight contiguous states. There is Michigan, waving at you in what's clearly the Northeast, and underneath it Ohio, leaning all the way into Pennsylvania. Minnesota and the Great Plains states are at least closer to the country's middle, but so are Oklahoma, and eastern Colorado, and not many people will go so far as to call those "the Midwest."

So then you think it's a kind of antiquated nickname that stuck. Once upon a time, the Old Northwest Territory—the places Congress sent Thomas Hutchins out to survey—*was* the frontier. It was the western reach of the U.S., so far as the thirteen states were concerned. It was the "fund," a huge reserve of land that needed to be mapped so we could sell it off. Then Jefferson made the Louisiana Purchase and "opened," as the historians' euphemism has it, these areas for settlement. Ohio and Indiana were now, still, *west*, but less west than previously, there being somewhat more America than before further beyond. As the course of empire moved westward, the same happened to Nebraska, and to Kansas, that hotbed of radical abolitionism. Once we had a *west*, our older, now-demoted west needed a new name.

There's something poignant about this folk etymology, in which the Midwest is a kind of abandoned frontier. You picture the whole region as a sort of once-shiny new mall marooned by suburban sprawl, left to crumble, only a few years after opening, in a no-longer-vital part of town. Such an image might help explain the sense of disappointment that grips so many of us here, the nostalgia for a moment that we can't quite pinpoint, the feeling not that things once were definitely better, but that they were *once understood to be on the verge, at least, of getting better.* A place that almost happened; a fund that almost prospered. That's how people in the town where I grew up seemed to feel about it—conversations full of regret for things that had almost happened, for the park that "they" *had been going* to build, for the downtown revitalization that "they" *were about to do* a few decades ago. It's the distinctive verb tense of what writer Mark Fisher, borrowing from Derrida, called "hauntology": the sense of being haunted by lost futures. As Fisher has argued, regarding post-Cold War life in general, it can feel here as though time has stopped but life has somehow continued.

"This Midwest," writes William H. Gass, in *In the Heart of the Heart of the Country.* "A dissonance of parts and people, we are a consonance of Towns. Like a man grown fat in everything but heart, we overlabor; our outlook never really urban, never rural either, we enlarge and linger at the same time, as Alice both changed and remained in her story."

"My parents didn't age, they simply sickened," Gass also wrote.

Small wonder, then, if those of us who live here—this dissonance of parts and people, of youth mysteriously aged— struggle to give any account of ourselves *as* Midwesterners.

After my Texas-born wife and I moved to Michigan—an eleven-hour drive in the snow during which time itself seemed to widen and flatten with the terrain—she pressed me into service as a local explainer, asking me about Midwestern customs, Midwestern cuisine, Midwestern identity. I struggled to answer her reasonable questions, about a region where I was born, and where I have spent most of my life, with anything more than clichés: bad weather, hard work, humble people. I knew these were inadequate. Connecticut winters and Arizona summers are also "bad"; the vast majority of humans have worked hard, or have been worked hard, for all of recorded history; and *humility* is one of those words, like *authenticity* or (lately) *resistance*, that serves mainly to advertise the absence of the thing named.

I soon learned that I was hardly the only Midwesterner left tongue-tied by the Midwest. Articulate neighbors, friends, colleagues, and students, when my wife asked them to describe their hometowns, replied with truisms that, put together, were also paradoxes: "Oh, it's in the middle of nowhere." "It's just like anywhere, you know." "We do the same things people do everywhere." No-places are as old as More's *Utopia*, but a no-place that is also everyplace and anyplace doesn't really add up. It's like a Zen koan, or a Platonic aporia. Yet people here will say all these things within a few sentences of each other, unconscious of any self-contradiction.

"Don't people say that anywhere?" was my response when my wife pointed this out to me.

People don't, in fact, talk like this everywhere. You don't hear this language from Southerners, Californians, or Yorkshiremen. Canadians live in a country that has been jokingly described as America's Midwest writ larger—Canada and our Midwest share, among other things, manners, weather, topography, and a tendency among their inhabitants to downplay their own racism—yet they are hyperspecific in their language, assuming a knowledge of local landmarks that it never occurs to them non-Canadians may not possess. They assume that whatever their setting is, it is *a setting*, not, as Glenway Wescott wrote of Wisconsin, "an abstract nowhere." And when I meet Southerners who grew up, as I did, in an obscure small town, they start by describing its peculiarities and local eminences, its affiliations and begats. They proceed—rightly—as though every place on earth were a Yoknapatawpha that hadn't yet found its

Faulkner. Whereas when I meet other former Midwestern farm town kids, they describe it by its proximity to an interstate, a university, a landmark: to something you'd see on a map. It's as if we're always seeing our places from two perspectives at once: our own, and then, overlain on our own memories like a transparency, Thomas Jefferson's grid.

Even Midwesterners' most self-critical tropes—the things we say when we're trying to rip off the mask of politeness—sound, on examination, like evasions. We like, for example, to castigate ourselves at length for our passive-aggressiveness. Ask Minnesotans about "Minnesota Nice"—the supposed propensity of Minnesotans to paper over all conflict with Nordic *bonhomie*—and they'll all condemn it with such ferocity, while disclaiming their own participation in it, that you have to wonder where exactly you'd have to go to find someone being Minnesota Nice. In my experience, Midwesterners are passive-aggressive to pretty much the same degree that many people in many places are. Any region will have its distinctive brew.

Similarly, any group of Midwestern white people will trip over each other trying to be the first to deplore the "whiteness" of the region. This is certainly at least a half-truth. The Northwest Ordinance of 1787 banned slavery in the region, though, as historian Tiya Miles has shown, elite Detroiters had owned slaves for generations under French rule, and the new American authorities found ways to grandfather it in after the ban. Later, escapees from Southern slavery often headed to the Midwest, but varying patterns of Fugitive Slave Law enforcement meant that they could never be too sure of their safety. (Dred Scott lived in Minnesota at the time he filed his famous lawsuit.)

And it's true, too, that many white Midwesterners imagine themselves as having avoided the issue, as living in places where black people just *happen not to have settled*. Growing up in a nearly all-white town, I gravitated toward this explanation: Why would black people, or anybody, *want* to live in Alma,

Michigan? (I certainly didn't.) But a little historical digging reveals the truth: the Midwest has never been simply white. We're a patchwork of disused Underground Railroad stations and former sundown towns, centers of black brilliance (Detroit, Chicago, Kansas City) and centers of Klan revival (Indiana). Barack Obama grew up here. Philando Castile was shot here. That's a history, even if a vexed one.

The same is true for other ethnic groups. Because we have a high historic concentration of German Lutherans and Catholics in places like Wisconsin and Minnesota, we also have a strong infrastructure for refugee resettlement—which means pockets of Somali, Hmong, and other populations in those states' cities. Latinx immigration has spiked in recent years, while white fascism has spiked in response. And the Midwest, like the country at large, was stolen from Natives, who are still very much here as well, adapting, thriving, resisting. The way we talk about Midwestern whiteness—a roll of the eyes and a shake of the head, as though we were discussing May snowstorms—risks turning this long dialectic of inclusion and exclusion, which can be changed, into a metaphysical fact that can't.

What all this suggests is that the Midwest is present in the minds of (some) Midwesterners as a huge blur, one that they lob descriptions *at* rather than describing. They claim big, vague virtues and accept big, diffuse blame. Their traits and virtues are simply those of *people*, of *Americans*. When they look at themselves, they see anyone.

If talking about the Midwest tires people out, writing about it is even harder.

An essayist declares: "The Midwest was always less distinctive than other regions." It "presents a blurry landscape," according to a reporter. Two of the region's most distinguished historians accuse it of lacking "geographic coherence." A team of psychologists cite it as a classic "fuzzy, probabilistic concept."

Even the smartest writers squirm and shift, looking for the right metaphor. Lincoln, in his Second Annual Address to Congress, called it "the great body of the republic." Teddy Roosevelt got specific: "the heart of true American sentiment." Over time, Roosevelt's image combined with the British geographer Halford Mackinder's 1904 coinage "heartland"— Mackinder's term for Central Europe—to create the idea of the Midwest as America's heartland, a place that is both a strategic center and a retreat from a too-complex world. Several decades and a million truck commercials later, Michael Martone rejected Roosevelt's metaphor: "I think of it more as a web of tissue, a membrane, a skin." I have yet to encounter the writer brave enough to call it America's genitals.

Leaving the human body aside, we find other metaphors, one of the most enduring being the sea: a sea of corn; a sea of grain. Marguerite Young, in *Miss MacIntosh, My Darling* (1965), puts a lovely spin on this trope:

> The scene, in fact, to one who was accustomed to a great body of water, was oceanic, dotted by pale pools in the vapors of mist, and I should not have been surprised to see, drifting over these empty, unmarked meadows of the first creation, something of the last, a cloud of pearl-breasted seagulls, all crying with angelic voices, or moored at some far, receding horizon, a lost ship which would never reach port.

For Young, the Midwest is a primordial ocean, a huge coil of pure possibility that swallows all forms, all possibilities. Her intentionally mixed metaphors—the "something of the last" that becomes a "cloud," then resolves into a cloud of seagulls who moor on the horizon, with "moored" giving the image the permission it needs to turn into "a lost ship"—embodies the protean nature of the ocean.

For Meridel Le Sueur, it was not one place, but every place:

> The Finns in the extreme north thought the forests, the severe winters, the inland sea, the deep mines, like Finland. The Norwegians discovered middle country pastures, forests, and deep streams like Norway's. The French found the St. Croix Valley in the Lake Pepin country as beautiful as the Greek and forests and broad rivers of France. Even the Dutch found inundated swamps bad enough to rival their own poor land.

Contemporary writer Nathan Beacom leaves earth behind completely: "[A]t night you feel that you are not looking at outer space but *in* it."

A body; a sea; a mirror; outer space. But the Midwest is also bare, humble, forgotten. Katy Rossing describes a common formula for writing about the region:

1. Begin with a loquacious description of the Euclidean-flat homogeneity of the landscape. This place looks boring. It looks like there's nothing here worth thinking about. . . .
2. In fact, it seems no one has really thought about it before, they all write. What IS the Midwest? The West, South, and East all have clear stories, stories that are told and retold in regionally interested textbooks, novels, movies. The Midwest? It's a humorously ingenuous, blank foil for another region. Example: *Fargo, Annie Hall.*
3. But wait a minute, the writers tell you, it turns out this place isn't empty at all!

This move, from flatness to emptiness to fullness hidden in plain sight, is incredibly common—I have not really escaped it. Yet the initial premise is only half-true. The Midwest isn't all flat. Think of the Driftless Area, where the glaciers never passed through with their vast, flattening bulk. And it's false in a deeper sense when it's meant, as it often is, to imply "boring." What flatness actually means is excess, overwhelm. By not hiding any of itself, a flat place exhausts your seeing. It gifts us more information than we can take in; dazed, bedazzled, we give up on it, and call our failure boredom.

We could take the concentration on flatness as a way of commenting on the similarity that capitalism has imposed upon the land. Jefferson's grid again: it made the country into square after square of liquidity, to be bulk-purchased and dedicated to this activity or that one, en masse, as capital dictates. (I wonder whether this bulk-purchasing constitutes one reason for the region's early success in manufacturing. A capitalist might simply buy himself a townsite and stick the factory wherever it needed to be, rather than trying to wedge a factory into an already-crowded Eastern townscape.) Boosters sometimes still call the region "America's breadbasket," even as climate change threatens to turn parts of the Great Plains into more or less the desert that eighteenth-century white travelers initially mistook them for. By the twentieth century it was America's foundry, and, during World War II, its armory. What all of this means in practice is vast visual repetition: mile upon mile of cornfields, block upon block of crumbling factories. (Willa Cather: "The only thing very noticeable about Nebraska was that it was still, all day long, Nebraska.")

But even used and battered landscapes have their particularity. Detroit's blight isn't Cleveland's blight isn't Gary's blight, any more than Manchester's is Birmingham's. Nor are any two cornfields truly exactly alike, despite Monsanto's best efforts. The British cultural imagination has been formed by writers like Hardy and Lawrence who are perfectly capable of distinguishing among bleaknesses; and some of the most interesting contemporary art and music consists of similar procedures repeated on a massive canvas. Surely we can learn to see in even the flattest, rustiest parts of the Midwest something richer than mindless repetition. (Also Willa Cather: "No one who had not grown up in a little prairie town could know anything about it. It was a kind of freemasonry.")

Rossing's formula for writing about the Midwest misses a few tricks. There must also be a resentful invocation of the term *flyover country* ("a stereotype," as one lexicographer points out, "about other people's stereotypes"). And one must end self-refutingly, by pointing out a number of examples of Midwestern achievement or importance, any of which—the frontier, populism, the Great Migration, farming, manufacturing—loom so large in the national discourse as to bring the article's initial premise into question.

In a 2015 essay for *Slate*, "The Rust Belt Theory of Low-Cost High Culture," reporter Alec MacGillis marvels at the cheapness—and, it seems, the mere presence—of good orchestras and museums in interior cities:

> The Cleveland Orchestra, one of the best in the world, offers a "young professional package," with regular concerts and special events, for a mere $15 per month—$20 for a couple. When I visited the St. Louis Art Museum, a monumental building deep within verdant Forest Park, I was stunned by its wealth of German expressionists (it has the world's largest collection of Max Beckmanns)—all for the entrance fee of $0. In Milwaukee, I spent hours

with my laptop at the café in the art museum's Calatrava-designed wing.

I appreciate MacGillis's enthusiasm, but why on earth is he so surprised? I suspect, rereading the passage, that he is not. MacGillis has done excellent work on Indiana and Ohio, and is himself a resident of Baltimore, another city that punches above its reputational weight. He is engaging in a kind of exquisitely light condescension that is well-known among Midwesterners, not the obvious kind practiced against them, but the subtle kind they practice back. "Oh, you'd be surprised how nice it is here! The newspaper is just top-notch!" they say, eyes wide as Dorothy Gale's, to the unbelieving New Yorker next them at the dinner party. "I just couldn't believe the museums!"

When a cultural commonplace establishes itself firmly enough, a writer sometimes has no choice but to feign surprise as he overturns it.

The Midwest is, in fact, constantly written about, often in a way that weirdly disclaims the possibility that it has ever been written about before. (After every election, journalism pledges itself to the Midwest as to a strict diet.) As some people spend their lives circling the same two or three epiphanies about themselves, announcing each one, each time, as though it had never before occurred to them, our reckoning with the Midwest is perpetually arriving, perpetually deferred.

Kate Soper, one of the most interesting contemporary composers, grew up in Ann Arbor. Our regional independent presses play important roles in literary history, or the literary present (Broadside, Lotus, Coffee House, Graywolf, Dzanc, Two Dollar Radio, Haymarket, Third World Press); writers as major as Toni Morrison, Louise Erdrich, Marilynne Robinson, David Foster Wallace, and Richard Powers set book after book in the region. If you took English in high school, you read—or pretended you'd read—Cather, Richard Wright, Gwendolyn

Brooks, Sherwood Anderson, Fitzgerald, Hemingway, Twain, Dreiser, Cisneros, all of whom wrote of the region lovingly or ambivalently; if you took it in college or graduate school, you may also have read Wescott, Roxane Gay, William H. Gass, David Hernandez, John Keene, Saul Bellow, Celeste Ng, Jaimy Gordon, Dinaw Mengestu, William Maxwell, Ana Castillo, August Derleth, Anne Carson, David Treuer, Jonathan Franzen, Grace Lee Boggs, Linda Hogan, Larry Woiwode.

If, on the other hand, your artistic interests run toward the visual or performative, the Midwest offers you Laurie Anderson, Grant Wood, Frank Lloyd Wright, Kerry James Marshall, Richard Hunt, Theaster Gates, Katherine Dunham, Second City, Steppenwolf, the Coen brothers. In the 1980s, as their cities shrank, Midwesterners dominated radio—Michael Jackson, Madonna, Axl Rose, Prince, Mellencamp. It gave the world prairie populism and progressivism, flawed as those were. It gave the world Abraham Lincoln, whom the South killed, and Fred Hampton, whom the FBI and Chicago police killed. It gave the world proto-punk and Motown, and so many weird little artists' collectives—Monster Roster, the Chicago Imagists, the Hairy Who, Destroy All Monsters, WARM.

These last examples point to the way that insularity—a term I don't intend as an insult—both serves Midwestern culture and blocks us from seeing it *as* Midwestern. In Andrea Lawlor's 1990s-set queer picaresque *Paul Takes the Form of a Mortal Girl* (2018), the protagonist, finding himself in the very city so many gay heartland kids dream of, turns his thoughts Midwestward:

> He'd expected San Francisco fashion to be more daring than that of Iowa City, but the [Iowa City] ped mall had been a nonstop fashion safari: punk rock drag queens and dyke hair fashion models and boy poets in tight polyester Sansabelts and all those rhetoric or painting graduate

students with their unpredictable fabric combinations. Maybe you had to be more inventive in the country; you had to learn to hem and rip and sequin, to sift through the cast-offs of the exotic manual laborers of middle America, those corn-husking teens, cereal factory third-shifters, and Monsanto janitors.

Midwestern creativity feeds on anonymity, on secrecy. It seam-rips at normality until it finds strangeness. We see Midwestern artists, then, as singular, not regional.

"In general," writes historian Andrew Cayton, "Midwesterners want to be left alone in worlds of their own making." This is a useful trait for artists. Think of the intensely self-aware Midwestern scenes that dot the landscape of American popular-music history like a series of private kingdoms: Motown; '70s Cleveland; '80s Minneapolis. Think of Tyree Guyton, whose masterwork is an entire Detroit neighborhood. Think of Prince, who famously shot down Matt Damon's attempt at conversation—"I hear you live in Minnesota"—with that wonderful remark, at once quintessentially Prince and quintessentially Midwestern: "I live inside my own heart, Matt Damon." The Midwestern artist hunkers on the landscape; she lives in her own heart.

But this lingering sense of hidden riches, of a cultural vitality not yet fully exploited or appreciated, brings to mind again that feeling that the Midwest is a thing appraised from elsewhere, a fund externally managed.

This Midwest: central but unseeable, discussed but undiscussable, unignorable but "ignored." Writers who attend to this paradox often attribute it to the territory's geographical fuzziness. But the word's history points in another possible direction.

I used to assume, again, that we call it "Middle" or *Mid-West* because it's the abandoned West that got left behind as the country expanded. This explanation feels plausible, and when you ask people where the term comes from, it's what they tend to say. In the 1980s, a geographer named James Shortridge decided to figure out whether it was true. "If this line of reasoning is correct," he wrote, "the phrase 'Middle West' likely would have had its origins in Ohio. . . . The time, perhaps, would have been the 1830s. As the settlement process continued, 'Middle West' would gradually have chased 'West' across the country." He did indeed discover that the term first appears in the 1830s—it's in a book by Timothy Flint.

So far, so good. Among scholars, Flint competes with James Hall, Daniel Drake, and Caroline Kirkland for the title of First Midwestern Writer. Along with that, he was an east-to-west migrator himself. Flint started his adult life as a clergyman from Massachusetts, but his sideline in amateur chemistry led his neighbors to accuse him of counterfeiting money—what else could he be doing with all those bottles? So he quit his job and turned missionary among the settlers of the Ohio and Mississippi Valleys, writing travel books and novels on the side until poor health forced him to write full-time. (His fictionalized biography of Daniel Boone is one reason that you still sort of know who Daniel Boone is, or feel you should know.) So Flint himself is in some sense a pioneer. Surely, if people in Ohio had coined the term "Middle West" in order to mark their own newly-only-part-of-the-way-west status, Flint would be the first to notice.

In fact, Flint used "Middle West" to describe . . . Tennessee. The first Midwestern writer didn't actually know he was a Midwesterner. No wonder we still can't decide which states count.

In using, and perhaps coining, the word, Flint seems to have been thinking up-down, not east-west, imagining the American West as though it were a layer cake with Tennessee in its center and North and South layers above and below.

There's reason to believe this was a common way of thinking about the area during the nineteenth century. Decades later, for example, when Lincoln described that "vast interior region," he saw it as the link between North and South: a thing between up and down.

After Flint, the term (per Shortridge) disappears from the record, turning up in the 1880s to mean Kansas and Nebraska, again in works by writers who are clearly thinking north-to-south rather than east-to-west. By the early 1900s, it's appearing all over the place, meaning basically what it means now—a huge, vague region stretching from somewhere around Buffalo or Pittsburgh to the-Great-Plains-Except-Probably-Not-Montana-or-Wyoming-Sorry.

Shortridge argues that the label stuck because, for so many people, it fit the *image* of this place, or these places: halfway between city and country, past and future. If Shortridge is right, then "Midwest" is a state of mind, or a name for a collocation of moods or tropes, some of them contradictory. It was "middle" in the sense that Benjamin Franklin prophesied when he wrote that the U.S., unburdened by an Old World class system, would reach a "happy mediocrity"—that in a settler democracy there would be no room for aristocratic pretensions or class stratification. Don't try to tell *me* what to do; five years ago you farmed muck like the rest of us.

And it's "middle" most of all in the way a middle-aged person is classically considered to be "middle": it's even-tempered, mature. It's no longer stupidly bold and unrefined like people in their twenties (that's Florida), nor grumpy and tetchy and neurotic and indolent like people in their sixties (that's Massachusetts). The Middle West is America aged just right. It's America in that golden moment we all look toward, when you've finally gotten yourself together but have plenty of future left to look forward to.

Probably nobody has done more to enshrine this idea of the Midwest as America's mellow maturity than Frederick

Jackson Turner, whose "The Significance of the Frontier in American History" (1893) proposed that as the frontier moved west, the same five stages of civilization played themselves out. It always started the same way: Native Americans and white frontiersmen disrupted by traders, who make room for pastoralists, who are followed by farmers and eventually farm towns, which yield to manufacturers and, finally, cities. At the time Turner wrote, some biologists thought that every animal relived the entire history of its evolution during the embryonic stage; you can see a similar dynamic here, with the whole evolution of civilization recapitulated over every patch of ground. This moving panorama, wrote Turner, "explains American development."

As Turner developed his ideas—which grew in influence just as the term "Middle West" in its now-received sense began to spread—he posited the region as a sort of buffer zone between old and new, a straw mattress on which Hamiltonian democracy might lie down with the Jeffersonian kind. "The task of the Middle West is that of adapting democracy to the vast economic organization of the present," he writes. Turner's argument positions the Midwest as a kind of permanent present looking just down the road at a raw future.

But if the Midwest is hard to describe, if it goes blurry as soon as we look at it, it does so in part because Turner was wrong. He created a national mythology in which the Midwest is our prosaic present, but its role in history, to start with, was future-oriented: a new fund of money to secure, then spend. As bank money flickers in time, existing simultaneously as your deposit (now) and the loan that draws interest (later), the Midwest has constantly played both future and past.

ROW 2

MAKING FUTURES IN THE MIDWEST

But that hoard of money couldn't be spent yet; people still lived in it. For the U.S. to secure its bag, Natives had to be removed, their still-thriving present made to look like an irrecoverable past. And Americans, having taken the land, had to rehearse new ways of living, and of getting a living, upon it.

We can't know what the ancient Mississippian people called the great city they erected, with a speed and a degree of apparent premeditation that one historian has called "visionary," in modern-day St. Clair County, Illinois. We know that they built mounds, grew maize, and had, as textbooks inevitably put it, an Extensive Trading Network. They made certain distinguishing sorts of trinkets and observed particular cultic practices; they followed a caste system. They left the place before 1350.

One thing we know for sure is that they did not call themselves, as we call them, Mississippians. Mississippi is a French mishearing of an Anishinaabe word for "Great River"; the Anishinaabe are not believed to have descended from the people that we have decided for some reason to call Mississippians; the place is called "Cahokia" because that's how the French heard the name of the tribe that was living there at the time they arrived, centuries later, a tribe that, asked who built all these weird mounds anyway, could not answer. History is a series of Borgesian mistakes.

The Ojibwe writer David Treuer has described the way his tribe found its way through the landscape: a precolonial tribal leader "dreamed that we should move west to where food grows on water." Lo and behold, Treuer points out, you can still buy Ojibwe wild rice all over the Midwest: food grown on water. In Lakota cosmology, the center of the world is the Black Hills of South Dakota, or at least that's what the Lakota name of the place translates to: "the heart of everything that is." (On the other hand, I love the idea that this could be a bit of ancient irony, like all the tiny, presumably joking Acmes and Apexes that dot the U.S. landscape now.)

Treuer's remark reminds us that for Plains Indians, as for all Natives, their history before European contact is a history of movements, changes, and slow but real technological innovation, like any people. When, centuries later, white settlers began to speak of a Corn Belt, the regions to which they applied the name were all places in which white settlers built upon centuries of excellent Shawnee farming practice. Further north and to the west, in Great Lakes country, Natives had managed the forest so as to attract better game (1000AD), domesticated corn, squash, and beans (ca. 1430AD), and built palisades (1500AD).

Contact with European capitalism and colonialism—two faces of one process—did to natives of the modern-day Midwest what capitalism always does: it created a pace of change that only owners and managers of capital could live with. (Think of English peasants, driven off their newly-enclosed lands to die en masse in newly crowded, smoky cities, all so some syphilitic aristocrat could get rich mass-producing socks.) Colonialism introduced the horse to the Plains Indians, who used it against each other with great viciousness, thus enriching European traders who profited from the carnage.

Further north, near the Great Lakes, British and Dutch traders sold the Iroquois enough weapons to guarantee hegemony. The intra-Native wars that resulted were "far more brutal than any known previously among these peoples," in the words of historian Richard White. Algonquian-speaking tribes resettled further east. As a result, by the time the French reached the area, they walked into a world so old, so broken, that it seemed to them new.

> The Frenchmen who traveled into the *pays d'en haute*, as they called the lands beyond Huronia, thought they were discovering new worlds. They were, however, doing something more interesting. They were becoming cocreators of a world in the making.

French colonialism was still *colonialism*, but, White argues, the French took, at least in that moment, a less dictatorial approach to their Native partners-in-worldbuilding than the English did. In nearly the same area as the Algonquian peoples that White writes about, the Anishinaabe were playing the French against the English in the fur trade so successfully that their numbers actually grew during the period from 1600-1800.

I stress this history, this complexity, in part because it belongs to the history and the present of the Midwest—even if that is the name of a much-later colonial culture's construct. I do so as well because it is still possible to find reputable historians peddling the lie that these places were more or less empty in 1787. They weren't a primordial land, a second Eden, waiting for white people; they had to be turned into that. A place can have a history; a fund cannot. A cleared lot has liquidity; an unmapped forest has less.

But I also do so to emphasize the scope of the problem that the fledgling United States government faced in turning those Northwest Territory lands into a liquid currency. When a government is trying to steal from people, that people's complexity and variety becomes a problem, and the effulgence of Native life in these lands had an effect on the American governing elite much like the one Samuel Johnson attributed to death: it concentrated the mind wonderfully. The future of the country seemed to hang on the new government's ability to clear all this life away.

But it was not inevitable that the United States would marshal the firepower, or the callousness, necessary to make this place into a fund. It was not inevitable that we would become the kind of country that, within a century, would let South Dakota Blackfeet die of smallpox while vaccines were available. The same brainpower and capital could have been applied to the far more interesting problem of generous coexistence—to the continuing "cocreation" of a joint world. People chose *this*, and built an army to make it happen.

If you read the debates that surrounded the ratification of the American Constitution, the thing that seems most surprising, from our vantage point, is this: a lot of people didn't want the U.S. to have a standing army. It ranked among the most popular arguments against a powerful central government. After all, why *would* you provide your rulers—those ambitious creeps—with a tool for seizing territory and enacting tyranny? Why would you prepare for war in the absence of the kind of unifying, immediate threat—invasion, dictatorship—that naturally arouses people to fight? Why would you fight a revolution and then immediately give your president what he needs to make him a king? And why would you do this when your worst enemy lay across an ocean?

So, at least, the arguments ran; and the first way that the Midwest shaped this country's future was to end them.

At the time Thomas Hutchins finished the Seven Ranges of Ohio, the surveying couldn't continue in that form. When, in 1787, Hutchins turned in his maps and the lengthy, detailed physical descriptions required by the ordinance, Congress had realized barely a hundred thousand dollars from its new "fund," and spent three times its budgeted amount on Hutchins's expeditions.

At the same time, powerful interests militated against the idea of leaving the land unsurveyed and unsold. Western plats offered congressmen, as representatives of the country, a chance to pay down war debt; to congressmen as individuals, they offered a chance to make money or accrue status through land speculation.

If a particular representative did not find these concerns pressing enough, he might consider the possibility—much mooted at the time—that white squatters and Native Americans might collude to keep Ohio Territory separate and independent. (This was not likely, as many squatters were virulently racist. You have to be to live on land that even your own government concedes to indigenes.) Rebellions such as Daniel Shays's had a similar effect. And the British were still encamped in the west, in violation of the Treaty of Paris, making little strategic overtures to the Great Lakes tribes.

In November 1791, Arthur St. Clair, the governor of the Northwest Territory, led a half-assed, underpaid army against Miami, Shawnee, and Lenape fighters, outfitted by the British. The Native generals Little Turtle and Blue Jacket handed St. Clair a defeat so pronounced as to earn a capital "D"—this is how it appears in the history books. Only twenty-four of his 1000-strong army escaped harm. If you wanted to demonstrate the theorem "These lands will make nobody rich until we have a disciplined army that answers to a central government," you could hardly do better.

At this point, George Washington's bill for a standing army had already squeaked through the House and was stalled in the Senate. Panic about St. Clair's Defeat, and Washington's promise to negotiate fairly with Natives, pushed it through. Washington then appointed, as major general of his army, a man already known by the sobriquet "Mad Anthony" Wayne, which must have raised some doubts concerning the seriousness of his will to negotiate.

Wayne trained his units carefully, and, over the course of the next four years, he secured the fund. He made his motley units into a fighting force, killed a great many Natives, and, with the decisive Battle of the Fallen Timbers, brought them back to the bargaining table. By 1795, writes historian William Hogeland, "America possessed not only a standing army but also national naval operations."

From that day to this, the United States—a nation naturally well-protected from foreign invasion—has continued to have both. For at least seventy years, they have been the most powerful on the planet.

To read the standing-army debates from the vantage point of 2020—to see how close we came to simply *not having one*— is like learning that Superman was originally meant to be a villain, or that Ronald Reagan once flirted with communism. In the contemporary U.S., no one can count all our military bases; worldwide dominion is the most fundamental fact of our common life, and its most fundamental distortion. American imperialism wastes money while lowering import prices; it deters enemies and creates them. (The Khmer Rouge arose from our bombing of Cambodia; ISIS from the chaos we made of Iraq.)

Most of all, it poisons our relationship to democracy itself. We are enjoined to thank veterans, and them alone, for the supposed ease of American life, as though the Voting Rights Act, or the eight-hour day, or the minimum wage, had been wrested from a foreign power by movie-handsome SEALS in the Pacific. The American civilian is made to feel a signatory to two social contracts: the democratic one we learn about in school, and the imperial one, in which our enlightened, humane way of life is an unsustainable bubble in a dark world, maintained by an organization that terrorizes its employees, crushes dissent, scorns vulnerability, intermittently practices torture, resents the Geneva Convention. We are encouraged to see democracy as something that can only live in a symbiotic relationship with authoritarianism. This relationship saddles us all—citizen and soldier—with guilt. The citizen pursues democracy with the sneaking suspicion that she merely cashes another's check; as for the soldier, well—she's taken human life, or failed to save it. Meanwhile, the American military ranks among the most prolific sources of carbon pollution in the world, unmaking our future even as it secures it. (And yet we hurry past homeless veterans on the street, eyes averted.)

To read the standing-army debates now is to feel you've been trapped in one of those time-travel dramas where the main character gets dropped into history moments before disaster occurs, and can do nothing but watch.

But life is not a movie. Every part of this was choice. It happened within a structure, a logic, but choice always does. It happened under immense pressure, but choice always does. The feeling that "Events have conspired to make this decision inevitable": that *is* one of the ways choice feels.

So what kind of country were we to be? Congress's decision to secure the Old Northwest Territory settled part of that question: an expansionist one. There still remained the question of what kind of life Americans would allow themselves in the places to which they expanded. They still had to decide, bluntly, how *nice* a place they would make for themselves to live here.

The survey of the United States' western lands began again almost immediately after the Battle of Fallen Timbers. Already, a few towns had been founded—Marietta was the first, in 1788—but now, with mapping underway in earnest, attention turned to the structure for land sales, settlement, and eventual statehood codified in the Northwest Ordinance of 1787. This law banned slavery in the territories and established the grid survey system, reserving some plats for veterans and others for schools. It obviously allowed individuals to buy land, but initially set prices and lot sizes to a level that—as compared, for example, with the 1784 Land Ordinance mentioned earlier, or the Homestead Act of 1862—advantaged (a) companies with a large pooled funds; (b) rich individuals, looking to invest rather than to homestead. "[T]he American settler found little within its provisions that was attractive," writes Roy M. Robbins of the ordinances. "The policy appealed more to speculators and men of money than to hardy yeomen." Even a historian sympathetic to the 1787 ordinance, Ray Allen Billington, admits that it was "adopted because of pressure from land jobbers." The terms changed over time to allow smaller parcels, but the initial emphasis was on corporate settlement.

This emphasis made a lot of people rich. The new places promised prosperous futures, after all. In Great Lakes Country, you had lakes on a scale unknown in Europe, older than the glaciers (though we didn't know about those yet), so vast that they had stayed ecologically "young," clear and fresh (big lakes age more slowly). Nearby you had forests and a flourishing trade in beaver pelts. Further west, thousands of miles of insanely fertile soil, and animals with even fuller and more valuable coats. (Trade had already driven most of the beaver out of the Great Lakes, in any case.) There was iron. There was a lot to touch, taste, enjoy. There was a lot to control, fence off, and sell.

For a long time, historians assumed that the U.S. originally had one manufacturing belt, in the Northeast, which traded with the Midwest for the food that we had a comparative advantage in producing. In this model, you'd find a pretext for clearing a particular area of Native Americans—pretexts that could always be found in the form of treaties signed by more-or-less random Natives (who had been lied to or paid off), or by isolated acts of Native violence that invariably triggered whole-village, scorched-earth white reprisal. And then you'd sell a square or two to some hardy would-be settler who had saved his pennies and was ready to start a farm. Towns would grow slowly but surely, because settlers needed others to trade, truck, and barter with, in Adam Smith's phrase. Gradually, a market accreted.

Geographers Brian Page and Richard Walker argue that this isn't how economic growth ever worked in the Midwest. Industries, they argue, *make* places, rather than picking from among preexisting sites. So the place was planned and settled in batches. Capitalists would buy several lots off Jefferson's grid at once, like a person dropping square after square of Jet's pizza onto their plate. *Here is an ideal place to smelt iron, but our factory workers will need a town, so let's go ahead and pick that up too while we're thinking of it. What about this patch over here, though—it's close enough to Cincinnati that we can sell to them. Perfect. Let's grab some of the surrounding area too and sell it to those hardscrabble types.* Towns often arose before settlers came to live in the surrounding hinterlands, rather than springing into existence as trading outposts for initially isolated farmers. Town, city, and countryside grew up together in a friendly or hostile symbiosis.

A new town always needs a little of everything, so agriculture, industry, processing, transit, and farm tech *also* grew up together. Cincinnati, for example, had already gotten rich milling flower by 1815. Midwesterners "developed the arts of agroprocessing to new heights," write Page and Walker. Hard Illinois soil drove John Deere to make a steel plow. The Midwest, having forced the issue of the country's military future, immediately became a model for its economic future.

Even the lack of amenities could force innovation: we got a nationwide movement for better roads in part because, in the 1880s, Midwestern dairy farmers couldn't drive their milk to the processing plant without the rutted, pitted roads jostling the stuff into clotting. Dairy farmers got collectively mad, and voila!—paved roads.

"In an earlier, more confident time, the Midwest was commonly held up as an example to the modern world of the true path to capitalist growth," conclude Page and Walker. Geographer Deborah Popper calls the region "an exercise in speculative and governmental property transfer." The cowtowns we drive past today, those bits of punctuation between cornfields: they were part of a bold, if too exclusive, experiment in human flourishing.

The people who got left out of this experiment were meanwhile aestheticized into myth. The notion of the Noble, Vanished Indian removed them from the realm of the imaginatively real as the army had removed them from the land. Local history-writing played its role in justifying the removal of Native Americans: as soon as a county had lasted long enough to deserve its own resident antiquarian, that writer would tell the story of the settlement's origins as a sort of quest in which settlers secured their right to the place by fighting. To ensure that the current residents were not seen as mere thieves, they would reinterpret the Native tendency to rotate predictably between places as a moral failure to "put down roots."

Funnily enough, the intensely commercial way in which the early Midwest was parceled out and sold also accounts for one of the region's weirdest, most lovably quixotic features—the fact that it's dotted with little abandoned utopias. Large pools of money are characteristic of greedy capitalism; they are also sometimes characteristic of groups of fanatical idealists who, like the early Christians, hold all things in common.

The most famous Midwest utopia is probably Harmony or New Harmony, Indiana, the site of *two* such attempts. Initially, the land was purchased, and, in 1814, the town was built by the followers of a German Pietist crank named George Rapp. The Rappites, like the pilgrims, fled Old World persecution—specifically, the government of Württemberg, which wanted them to baptize their children in the expected way. Relocated to Indiana, they delved and spun, threshed and made wine, in comparative peace, while holding all property in common, like the early Christians, and, unlike them, abstaining even from married sex. (Rapp had a biological son, conveniently conceived before the Spirit had explained to Rapp about the whole celibacy thing. This son later died in an accident, and the Rappites were dogged by rumors, apparently unfounded, that George had had the poor kid castrated.)

Contemporary Americans are raised to scorn the idea of utopia, especially if it involves the abolition of private property. But the Rappite version of Harmony was a success—visibly far more prosperous than its neighbors; the home of one of the first decent research libraries in America; so well-organized that nearby townspeople feared impending political domination by this clique of cheerfully blue-balled Germans. It didn't "fail." After about a decade, the Spirit explained to Rapp via the Book of Revelation that the community was needed back East, so he simply sold his town and started a new one, Economy, near Pittsburgh. From the outside, their movements appear simply erratic; you wonder, when reading about them, whether Rapp had involved his followers in a sort of improvised story and needed to generate plot twists, a drive he experienced as genuine and overwhelming religious conviction emerging from intense Bible study.

In any case, Rapp's town found a buyer in Robert Owen, the Welsh industrialist and social critic, a man easily as crazy as Rapp but militantly secular. Indeed, Owen's life and thought serve as an illustration of the porousness of this boundary. Owen had already scandalized England by writing *A New View of Society* (1813), a deeply strange book in which Owen claims to have discovered the errors that corrupt human nature, and then doesn't really tell you what they are. It resembles nothing so much as one of those interminable "here's the one weird trick for how I lost belly fat" audio commercials of the mid-2010s internet, describing the inevitable soon-to-come social impact of a secret, the disclosure of which is promised and promised and never given. His secret has something to do with rationality and with education—the book's clearest claim is that humans are so totally a product of their environment that they cannot be praised or blamed for their mistakes. All you can do, if you don't like their behavior, is to teach them better. (One wonders whether Owen applied this belief to himself, if he asked, *Who taught me this?*, and in this way created a world-devouring logical paradox.)

In some areas, this philosophy made him, for his time, a genuine humanitarian—Marguerite Young, chronicling the two Harmonys, wrote that "who fails to love this man, fails to love humanity." He offered free schooling to the children of his factory town, New Lanark, Scotland, rather than making them mill, and he gave their parents an eight-hour day, as Henry Ford would do eighty years later for the beleaguered parents of Detroit schoolchildren. Instead of shouting at his workers, or sexually exploiting the women, he would simply give them data reflecting their performance, like an efficiency consultant, or like one of those terrible, "innovative" apps that sends your long-suffering school-age children a text message every time they get a grade below an A. Owen had a terrifying managerial streak, as this example shows—he was the type drawn to socialism because he thought it *efficient*, not because he thought it moral. He spent his final years, the 1850s, still trying to outwit humanity, in this case by inventing a sort of rolling arson machine so destructive that its mere existence would frighten everyone out of fighting wars. Who loves this man fails to love humanity.

In any case, Owen's attempt to replicate the success of New Lanark in America failed. He bought Harmony, renamed it New Harmony, and then left on a speaking tour. His son Robert Dale Owen managed, or mismanaged, in his absence. By 1827—three years after Owen purchased the town from Rapp—the New Harmony experiment in paternalist socialism was dead. In 1940, Young, traveling through it, saw only "a filling station where there were two utopias, Mr. Babbitt where there was an angel."

New Harmony lives, however, in the culture's memory, in part because you can look at it and see so many of the tropes about America, religion, the rise of capitalism, and other things that textbook writers like to talk about prefigured. If Weber argued that intense, otherworldly religious devotion made Calvinists rich, and in turn that wealth made their descendants worldly but no less sober, and thus did the world become an iron cage—well, here is a religious communist town that got rich and went secular. Harmony (IN) led straight to Economy (PA). If, instead, we want to think of America, or the Midwest, in terms of unfulfilled utopian promises, we read Young, and we sigh over the angel displaced by Babbittry. But nineteenth-century utopians saw their communities not as impractical retreats from history but, as historian Arthur Bestor writes, as "guides and pathfinders to the future." They were able to live so unusually because they believed, as ardently as any Elon Musk, that what they did was inevitable, was common sense.

Later, the Abolitionists, when they rushed to places like Kansas and Ohio and Iowa to build new institutions and societies on antislavery principles, also acted on an impulse that we should call utopian—not in the sense of "impossible place," but in the sense of "exemplary place." When the followers of Theodore Weld, wrought-up by several days of intense academic debate and religious revival (activities that the early Midwest did not see as separate), took over Cincinnati's Lane Seminary and threatened to turn it into a center of anti-slavery activity, he acted as a "utopian" in this sense. So did the founders of Brooklyn, Illinois, the first all-black town in America—a town founded on the idea, surely as radical in the nineteenth century as communism, that black Americans could be free.

A utopia acts as a rudder on the future: it provokes friction, inconvenience, wonderment, bending the world ever so slightly more its way. Writes Bestor: "The small, voluntary, experimental community was capable . . . of reconciling [between] apparently divergent aims: an immediate, root-and-branch reform, and a peaceable, nonrevolutionary accomplishment thereof. A microcosm of society . . . could undergo a drastic change in complete harmony and order, and the great world outside could be relied upon to imitate a successful experiment without coercion or conflict." This is the impulse anyway. So radical democratic politics, as well as capitalist ambition, placed towns on the map of the Midwest.

In fact, this utopian impulse precedes even the Rappites. Marilynne Robinson credits it to Eastern Puritans whose descendants turned that movement's moral earnestness not to material success—as in the Max Weber thesis—but to abolitionism and other forms of radical politics. It had at least one other source as well. Late in the first decade of the nineteenth century, a group of religious idealists poured into Fort Greenville, and then, following further revelations from their prophet-leader, to another place in the territory that would soon be known as Indiana. They, like the later Rappites, were animated by an idea, a vision of life, and they sought to build a self-sufficient town where that vision could be realized in practice. Their leader saw himself as restoring long-forgotten and neglected religious principles, but, in doing so, they built something new—just as the Puritans, in seeking to restore the practices of what they imagined to be the early church, had created an intellectual and political vanguard. And like the Puritans—like anyone who seeks reform, purification, perfection—they were called fanatics. Their intellectual lineage, too, did include some discrediting excesses: a witch-burning here and there. They certainly believed in miracles and claimed to do them.

I am describing, of course, the Shawnee followers of Tenskwatawa. He was, earlier in the decade, a town drunk who, sometime around 1805, emerged from a deep sleep with a vision of Pan-Indian reform and resistance. His reputed history as a ne'er-do-well probably only added to the seriousness of the occasion; it marked the difference between his old and new selves. In his vision, the Maker of Life (or Breath, in some translations) showed him a gameful and fruitful land, an earthly paradise, and in one part of it, a wigwam that held the souls of sinful Indians who were subjected to Dantean punishments. (Alcoholics were forced to drink molten lead, for example.)

The Maker of Life told Tenskwatawa that all tribal divisions among Natives were over: Indians "are now but one." His vision also revealed to him that Indians could mix no more with white people, who had been created by an evil spirit. Here we can see an anticipation of another Midwestern religious visionary, Nation of Islam founder Wallace Fard, who in 1930s Detroit taught that whites were the creation of an evil demigod.

Tenskwatawa sought to unite all Native Americans as a single group. His more famous brother, Tecumseh, turned his vision into a military plan.

For decades (white) historians saw Tenskwatawa as a fraud and a failure. It's true that he lost face with his own people after launching a major battle, the Battle of Tippecanoe, too early. Here he was defeated by another leader history remembers as a failure, or as a *Jeopardy!* question: Northwest territorial governor William Henry Harrison, who in time became the first Midwestern president, though not for long. (He got caught in the rain and died thirty-one days into his term.) More recent historians, in any case, see Tenskwatawa not as the last-ditch flail of a faltering race, but as the spiritual leader of a sincere and sophisticated movement, one that, whatever else, helped to create the idea of Native Americans as a unified people.

In this, recent historians are simply deferring to the judgment of the prophet's contemporaries. A Shaker visitor to Fort Greenville wrote in 1846 that "We felt as though we were among the tribes of Israel, on their march to Canaan." Even Thomas Jefferson, Tenskwatawa's enemy, acknowledged him as a reformer, and Prophetstown, the city he built in Indiana, was briefly the biggest city in the Northwest Territory—bigger even than Cincinnati.

What would the history of the Midwest, of America, be, if Tenskwatawa had succeeded? If Washington, D.C., had needed to negotiate with a single native nation united behind one leader? Would we have had to adopt something closer to a Native land ethic, treating land as a shared resource? Would we—whatever unimagined hybrid *we* exists in this scenario— have been happier? It's an impossible question not to ask, and also meaningless. Nobody that you know or I know—Native or other—would exist in that timeline.

Yet in another sense, Tenskwatawa *did* win. The concept of "*The* Indian" owes a lot to him; by helping to create a kind of pan-Indian political project, he made possible the inter-tribal cooperation that has underwritten Native resistance and survival ever since. His existence makes it easier to imagine Sitting Bull's bravery, the American Indian Movement, the Standing Rock protests. A prophet predicts, and so sets in motion, a future; and Tenskwatawa was at least some sort of prophet.

Meanwhile, the Midwest yoked itself to the idea of the future in another way: it gave birth to many of our ideas and methods for controlling the future, for making it, like land, habitable, for making it, like the trains of a proverbial fascist state, run on time.

Once again, for this to happen, a native future had to get knocked off the board. This one was Black Hawk's. When, in the early 1830s, the U.S. government decided to enforce a stipulation in an illegal 1804 treaty that required Natives to live on the west bank of the Mississippi River, he called bullshit. According to Black Hawk's *Autobiography*, that treaty had itself been signed by a group of drunk men, who didn't know what they were signing, and one of whose friends had been taken hostage. When, in 1816, the 1804 treaty was reaffirmed in the agreement that Black Hawk and other Native fighters signed after siding with the British in the War of 1812, he had been misinformed about its contents. (These anecdotes give some idea of what Natives had to deal with when they resorted to civilized diplomacy.) So he gathered a pan-Indian community and headed for Illinois to establish an armed settlement on ancestral lands. He wrote:

> My reason teaches me that *land cannot be sold.* The Great Spirit gave it to his children to live upon, and cultivate, as far as is necessary for their subsistence; and so long as they occupy and cultivate it, they have the right to the soil—

but if they voluntarily leave it, then any other people have a right to settle upon it. Nothing can be sold, but such things as can be carried away.

His argument is so old it sounds new.

Territorial governors chased his group off the land, killed many of them, and took others prisoner, including Black Hawk himself, who narrated these words from captivity. These soldiers returned home with a vision of their own: the fabulous fertility of the area known in the Miami-Illinois language as "Checagou," land of wild garlic. Many Potawatomi, who had not joined Black Hawk's group, still lived in that land, and they too were gradually pushed off by a combination of violence and fraud. By 1836, it was a city of four thousand people, mostly white.

That city would pioneer the purchasing of futures—futures made simple, movable, scrubbed of local fauna, easily compelled—in a third sense. Chicago's weather is notoriously cold and unpredictable, and transporting your wares could get ugly. If the river froze too early in the year, you could store your stuff, but then in the spring you'd face a glut and low prices because everyone else did the same thing. Writes Emily Lambert in *The Futures*:

> So river merchants started arranging to sell the corn in advance. Someone said, "Hey, I know it's cold and only March now, but I'll deliver three thousand bushels of corn to you next June for a penny cheaper than what you'd pay me today. Deal?"

Chicagoans drove this new trade, which quickly became a trade in *guesses about the future*. "By the mid-1850s, a single contract could pass through several hands before finally ending up in the hands of a merchant who wanted corn," Lambert writes.

At the same time, the invention of the grain elevator hastened wheat's transformation from solid commodity to abstract index of value—from product of land to part of the fund. The advantage of these elevators was that you didn't have to carry all your wheat in giant sacks all the time. But without the sacks, how could you tell whose wheat was whose, and who gets paid when a bushel sells? The Chicago Board of Trade, initially a crackers-and-cheese social club, provided a solution to this problem in the form of its wheat grades. All wheat of a certain quality got dumped into the proper section, and the farmer got a receipt, which he could use as though it were currency. Grain stopped being just a thing you ate and became a kind of money. The biodiversity of farms thinned out: what kind of fool would grow a variety that *didn't* count as money?

In early years, the Board, where this new trade in futures took place, got crowded and messy. To solve this problem, they built a kind of amphitheater-like structure so that people could see each other, and clocks overhead that tracked prices through the day. Everyone called it the Pit. In Frank Norris's 1903 novel of the same name, a young woman, leaving the opera, glimpses it:

> Laura looked, suddenly stupefied. Here it was, then, that other drama, that other tragedy, working on there furiously, fiercely through the night, while she and all those others had sat there in that atmosphere of flowers and perfume, listening to music. Suddenly it loomed portentous in the eye of her mind, terrible, tremendous. Ah, this drama of the "Provision Pits," where the rush of millions of bushels of grain, and the clatter of millions of dollars, and the tramping and the wild shouting of thousands of men filled all the air with the noise of battle! Yes, here was drama in deadly earnest—drama and tragedy and death, and the jar of mortal fighting. And the echoes of it invaded the very

sanctuary of art, and cut athwart the music of Italy and the cadence of polite conversation, and the shock of it endured when all the world should have slept, and galvanised into vivid life all these sombre piles of office buildings.

Norris's language, horror-struck as it is, also calls up associations familiar to any reader of the naturalist literary tradition he worked in. The Pit is immense, frightening, a terrible pagan god, but it's also *life* as post-Nietzsche intellectuals understood it, an ungentle Darwinian scrum that overwhelms polite traditions like opera and being kind. Look at a heart: fleshy, obscene, excessive. A heartland cannot only be even and flat.

Utopia, it seems, was off the table.

ROW 3

CHANGES IN THE LAND

As we've seen, Midwestern historians dispute the common-sense idea that our towns and cities grew "organically" from a Frederick Jackson Turner-style accretion of small settlements. Historian William Cronon points to Chicago, in particular, as an example of the ways that this wasn't true. He quotes an 1840 historian who describes "a chain almost unbroken of suppositious villages and cities"; Chicago itself began as one of these paper towns.

A certain kind of speculator always fancies himself an intellectual. (The pronoun is intentional.) Think, in our own era, of the way that Enron executives appealed to Richard Dawkins's *The Selfish Gene* when they wanted to fire people, or of financier-pedophile Jeffrey Epstein's well-maintained collection of physicist buddies. American speculators of the 1830s kept up with the latest European science, and feverishly theorized about which places would have the "right" range of temperatures to host the, well, *sorts of persons* most intrinsically capable of "advanced" civilization. (They assumed Europeans, of course.) One charming school of thought held that you could predict future patterns of settlement by extrapolating from the way planets cluster around stars. People with money and prestige *believed* that there would be a Chicago-like object on the landscape sooner or later; the only question was where. Galena? Vincennes? Mighty Cleveland, with its nearby lake? Whoever guessed right controlled the future.

Chicago became Chicago, in Cronon's telling, by a series of happy accidents and minor advantages. He lists "cheap lake transportation to the east" and early friendliness toward railroads among these advantages. But most of all it was the railroads. The American mythology and iconography of railroads is studded with references to the Midwest, from "Rock Island Line"—a folk song that began as an advertising jingle, which then gave its name to one of the loveliest novels ever written about Iowa—to the James Brothers, who staged their first robbery on that same line, in 1873; from Casey Jones (an Illinois Central operator) to Howlin' Wolf's "Smokestack Lightnin.'" Meridel Le Sueur quotes an anonymous worksong that reflects this moment, the laborer freed to wander the inland ground from job to job:

> *You advertise in Omaha*
> "Come, leave the valley of the Kaw."
> Nebraska calls, "Don't be misled,
> We'll furnish you a feather bed."
> Then South Dakota lets out a roar,
> "we need 10,000 men or more,
> Our rain is turning, prices drop,
> For God's sake save our bumper crop!"
> In North Dakota, I'll be darn,
> The wise guy sleeps in a Hoosier barn,
> The Hoosier breaks into his snore,
> Then yells it's quarter after four.
> Oh, harvest land, sweet-burning sand,
> As on the sun-kissed field I stand,
> I look away across the plain

And wonder if it's going to rain.
I vow by all the brands of Cain
That I will not be here again.

Reading this, you almost feel that the transcontinentals made a new kind of consciousness possible, a sense of oneself as a wanderer, not over the relatively small territories encompassed by a walker, but over the imaginative map of an entire landmass. The power, and loneliness, of traveling on a map, not a territory. On the other side of the singer's angry vow—"I will not be here again!"—is that unnameable melancholy one feels on Midwestern road trips, driving through those towns that seem mirror images of one's own: *I have always been here; I have never been here; I will never be here again.*

In retrospect, the railroads' development looks inevitable, but Richard White—their greatest contemporary historian, and, not accidentally, one of the leading authorities on the history of the Midwest and West as well—points out that the massive transcontinentals didn't actually *need* to happen when or how they did. America could have waited, at least:

> . . . regional lines in California and the Midwest could have handled most of the productive traffic. Rail lines connecting Chicago, Kansas City, and St. Louis with the lands east of the ninetieth meridian would have allowed the settlement of the prairies, and other lines connecting California and western Nevada with San Francisco Bay would have created a sufficient Pacific rail network.

The transcontinentals, like those "supposititious villages" that didn't fail, were a vision willed into reality by speculators, a massive, unwieldy idea *made* profitable by a combination of old-fashioned corruption and a dreamlike conviction of their eventual profitability. Think of the way, in our own lifetimes, Amazon lost money year after year, while seeming so thoroughly futuristic that politicians and investors have made objectively bad decisions (imposing no sales taxes on online sales for decades, for example) simply because they fear the consequences of disobeying a not-yet-entirely-real thing that nevertheless sits out ahead of us so solidly that it seems to bend the present toward itself.

Or turn your eyes to England, the mother country, where the transition to coal-powered steam engines looked similarly "inevitable" to the people who lived through it. Ecologist Andreas Malm has shown that, during the period when mill owners switched from waterwheel power to steam, the former was *actually the better choice*—probably cheaper, certainly more reliable and abundant, and capable of generating comparable power. This was true at least into the 1850s. The owners liked coal-powered steam engines better, even though they were economically a "worse" idea, because, for a variety of reasons, those engines made it easier to control your *workforce*. (Taking the politics out of "political economy" and turning it into just "economics," that apolitical science, was a stupid idea.)

Or take whatever piece of idiotic tech, soon to fail, that someone is selling your boss as you read this.

Even those of us who distrust capitalism often see in its machinations the inevitability of gravity, when its history is more like the self-fulfilling power of a terrible but memorable dream. That was true of early Chicago, of the mid-1830s land speculation boom that so fueled Midwestern growth. And it was *definitely* the nineteenth-century railroads, which made the Midwest, metaphorically, a "heart," a hub at the center of a system of circulation.

A thing about railroads: they are *very, very expensive*, and once you build one, you are locked in. In this way they resemble the grain elevators that revolutionized Chicago's economy and made futures trading on a large scale possible. Once they exist, even if you had no intention of dealing with them, they maintain such a massive presence on the horizon that you may have to change the way you work in order to accommodate their elephantine whims.

The fixed costs of construction, fuel, permits, and whatnot eat so much of your money that you can't simply refuse to provide services when, as will sometimes happen, the cost of those services dips beneath the level of today's expenses. "The simple but paradoxical fact was this," writes Cronon: "when railroad business was poor, a company had to attract traffic—even when that traffic did not pay the cost of its own transportation. Since the company was going to pay fixed costs no matter what, earning something was better than earning nothing." If you operate at a loss, you can at least staunch some of your own bleeding, service some of today's debt. So the railroads, once built, ran more or less on time, at least until they failed entirely.

Riverboat operators didn't do that. Stagecoach operators didn't do that. They could stall their journey until prices leveled out and the journey seemed likely to be worth it; early nineteenth-century travel writing describes wait times that make our Christmas airport horror stories sound almost civilized. So fixed costs meant fixed schedules, fixed timetables. The future—next week, next month, next year— began to straighten out like a highway, instead of bending and meandering like a walking trail.

And prairie farmers, as I've mentioned, standardized their treatment of the land, too, to participate in this predictable system, raising only those plants that sold reasonably well in *any* market. (You can't blame them: farming ranks with day labor, parenthood, and freelance writing among the occupations most harassed by sheer happenstance, by the recalcitrance of the future in the face of our hopes. Any bit of certainty you *can* seize, you will.) The rich variety of prairie life thinned out into the endless rows of identical strains of corn and wheat that we see today.

And all this to participate in a system so shaky that it seized and panicked every few years at best. "Failures," writes White, "were the lifeblood of the transcontinentals." And failing as they went, they became the prototypes of that modern American corporate consciousness—amoral, stupid, but sanctimonious, always demanding either its eminent domain rights or its bailout—that we now send kids to business school to learn. Matthew Josephson's classic *The Robber Barons* (1962) quotes a member of California's 1878 Constitutional Convention, who described one railroad baron as follows:

> They start out their railway track and survey their line near a thriving village. They go to the most prominent citizens of that village and say, "If you will give us so many thousand dollars we will run through here; if you do not we will run by." And in every instance where the subsidy was not granted this course was taken, and the effect was just as they said, to kill off the little town.

The railroads were not powerful because they were profitable. They were granted the time to become profitable because they knew how to wield power.

Their ability to shape the Midwest's future, and to change the velocity with which that future approached, is often summarized in terms of their power to destroy the physical environment. Railroads made logging on a massive scale possible—with the result that deforestation became, according to biologist Nancy Langston, "the first great issue in the American environmental moment." More famously, they made possible the near-extermination of the Plains buffalo. Railroads fed demand for buffalo hides back east, and the laborers building track required good, cheap, local food, which buffalo themselves provided. Most depressingly, perhaps, the railroads made it possible for large groups of costumed bourgeois to travel to the Plains and pretend to be English sportsmen.

Some railroads ran special deals where you could even hunt without leaving the train. The engineer would slow down whenever a herd of bison approached the tracks, and you'd just climb to the roof and take potshots, like the worst sort of playable character in the worst sort of video game. It's manly, like downing moose from a helicopter. Among charismatic large animals, bison are particularly easy to kill because when you shoot one, others gather around it, as though in mourning. Stupid and noble, they present a fat target.

The least important aspect of that tragedy was the harm it inflicted on the character of the hunters themselves, though this harm boggles the imagination. The near-destruction of a species matters far more. But consider: Military authorities encouraged this destruction because it helped them clear the area of Native Americans who ate buffalo. "Kill every buffalo you can! Every buffalo dead is an Indian gone," one soldier is quoted as saying. When we talk about the near-extinction of the noble bison, as though we simply regretted the loss of a picturesque animal, we ignore an even uglier project at work: oppression of Native Americans. Having lost a source of self-sufficiency, Plains Indians were easier to force onto reservations; those who rebelled tended to end up like Crazy Horse.

The linked attacks on buffalo and Plains Indians reminds us that conservation is never simply about the protection of pretty views and interesting animals. No—when someone tells you that the needs of The Economy are in conflict with The Environment, with the usual implication that we must sacrifice views to dollars and places to funds, what they are usually saying is that the needs of *some people who want to get richer* are in conflict with the needs of *some other people who want to stay alive.* The ecocide of the Plains buffalo was simultaneously the intentional destruction of a Native economy.

Reading American history, it is easy to feel as though the tremendous moral energies aroused by the Second Great Awakening simply disappeared in the 1860s. The Abolitionists—a group so patently noble, and so breathtakingly effective (if only in making the Civil War inevitable), that much of the subsequent historiography about the movement, painting them by turns as Yankee interlopers or proto-white-liberals-in-the-bad-sense, seems like an effort to smother a good example—disappear from the scene, or waste their energy banning alcohol. Having rightfully lost a war—and how often, in the long history of human conflict, can one say with such certainty that the right side lost?—the South sets about winning the peace, and the North just *lets them do it.* The country seems to lose its soul overnight, like an idealistic college friend two weeks after Goldman Sachs hired him.

But reformist energy gathers again, and in a transit-crazed country, it gathers mostly by the side of the road. Between the 1870s and the 1920s, the Midwest was swept by the Granger, Populist, and Progressive movements in turn, all of which challenged, among other things, the monopolistic power of the railroads.

In a historical moment characterized, again, by speed and by changes in the pace of change itself, it is interesting to note that Charles Francis Adams characterizes the first of these movements precisely in these terms. Writing in 1875, Adams—brother of Henry, grandson of John Quincy, great-grandson of the second president, *railroad executive*—describes the Grangers as silly youths:

> In the first place we have a young agricultural community, which has grown up with unprecedented rapidity in the very center of the continent, many hundreds of miles away from those great centers of industry to which it must look for its markets and sources of supply. . . . New social organizations cannot enjoy that accumulation of knowledge, of education, and of political habits which is found among people of the same race but of an older civilization; to look for it is as unreasonable as to look for an equal degree of wealth. . . . They thus see an evil, a wrong, with great clearness; seeing it thus, feeling it thus, they go directly at its most obvious manifestation, and do not often stop to look for a hidden cause.

The Grangers, to put it simply, were farmers, many of them Midwestern, who advocated first for more railroads, and then for less usurious terms for the loans that some of their communities incurred in building those railroads, lower delivery prices (from railroad operators), and lower storage prices (from grain elevator operators). Adams, attempting to defend them against what he saw as Eastern condescension, still frames them as unsophisticated fellows in a hurry, who thus fail to attack the root of the problem. A community organizer might respond that you cannot address root causes until you build a collective subject capable of naming its problems and attacking them head-on. And the Grangers scored several major victories: free rural delivery of mail, some road improvements, and most impressively, an 1877 Supreme

Court decision that grain elevators, even if privately operated, were subject to public regulation because of their importance. This was an important principle, and if the Supreme Court soon overturned it, that was *their* screwup.

Adams gestures, though without realizing it, at an important failure of the Granger, Populist, and Progressive movements in his phrase "of the same race but of an older civilization." These movements were largely white; indeed one goal of the Grangers was to reunite Northern and Southern farmers through common cause. (Though this could cut both ways: many small Southern farmers were black, and the threat of a union between poor whites and poor black Southerners seemed active enough to motivate centuries of strategizing on the part of Southern elites.) So the Grangers, for example, failed to expel Southern chapters that practiced segregation or opposed black farmers' interests (including even such basic human rights as the ability to vote). Thus does the unexamined, automatic solidarity between white people—the instinct that ignores another person's racism because "we have to stay united," or, today, "things are too polarized"—undermine American reform, generation after generation.

But the Populists, a direct outgrowth from the Grangers, both maintained and broadened their political project. In addition to calling for an income tax, worker collective bargaining, and fiat money—treating money as a pragmatic tool for extending buying power, which it is, and not as an unalterable metaphysical reality—they initially attacked the Democrats over Jim Crow and envisioned a coalition of the poor of all races. (They did show a bit of a weakness for conspiracy theories involving Jews and banks—how much of a weakness, historians still debate.) This multiracial solidarity was a promising development.

Nearly 130 years later, it . . . remains promising, as beautiful and elusive things do. Its near-appearance among Midwestern crowds at Jesse Jackson's presidential rallies in 1988 threw the Democratic Party's elites into a panic from which they have yet to recover. The whiff of it lent moral grandeur to the presidency of Barack Obama for years after he had made his true priority—to stand between the billionaires and our pitchforks—explicit. For a suffering person to prioritize someone else's needs, someone else's injustices, requires a moral genius that is not common in any demographic; but a sufficiently dogged communicator can remove, for a while, the illusion that they are, in any real sense, somebody *else's*.

Progressivism, a national movement with strong ties to the Midwest, concerned itself more directly with the future. A modern economy required certain adjustments, so that America might continue to progress along some assumed timeline. But the movement looked at its moment from two perspectives at once: that of managers, and that of workers. Too often the managerial view won out; Progressives could be like Robert Owen, embracing some humane policies merely because they thought them efficient. Some Progressives' enthusiasm for "modernizing" human reproduction as well—by sterilizing undesirable people—is precisely, and ironically, what renders this movement a distasteful curio to so many today.

Henry Ford, the weirdest man of the twentieth century, gives off a faint but unmistakable whiff of the prairie progressive. He shares their obsession with efficiency, and he has the style down pat. His autobiography (ghostwritten, but sounding like him), which bears the ostentatiously aw-shucks title *My Life and Work*, somewhat resembles a Teddy Roosevelt stump speech, all showboating plainness and bustle. For example:

I am not a reformer. I think there is entirely too much attempt at reforming in the world and that we pay too much attention to reformers. We have two kinds of reformers. Both are nuisances. The man who calls himself a reformer wants to smash things. He is the sort of man who would tear up a whole shirt because the collar button did not fit the buttonhole. It would never occur to him to enlarge the buttonhole.

To which the reader can only respond: Dad, calm down.

But as this passage shows, Ford thought of himself as a conservative, a good farm boy. (Though "even when very young I suspected that much might somehow be done in a better way.") He saw both his cars and his industrial methods as "a powerful integrator," writes Greg Grandin. He believed that they would sow cohesion and conformity among scattered Americans:

[T]he rational application of technology would allow for the holistic development of industry and agriculture; the tractor and other advances in mechanization would relieve the treasury field and barn, the car and truck would knit regional markets closer together . . .; radios and telephones would overcome rural isolation.

Anyone who lives in the world Ford made can confirm that cars don't glue; they break. So does the assembly line, where Ford regularly sped up production to a degree not really sustainable for normal humans. Doing the same thing all day long causes social breakdown and misery, a fact Ford might have figured out by reading Adam Smith, that praiser of pin factories:

The man whose whole life is spent in performing a few simple operations, of which the effects are perhaps always the same, or very nearly the same, has no occasion to exert his understanding or to exercise his invention in finding out expedients for removing difficulties which never occur. . . . But in every improved and civilized society, this is the state into which the laboring poor, that is, the great body of the people, must necessarily fall unless the government takes some pains to prevent it.

You can hear Ford starting up at that mention of government intervention: "Do *what* now?"

In lieu of improving workers' conditions beyond the strict limits he felt appropriate, he maintained an equally efficient union-busting spy network, headed by the notorious sociopath Harry Bennett. And having conquered the world—at least until other Midwestern automakers hit upon the idea of offering consumers choices—he could think of little to do but impose his imagined version of small-town Midwesternness upon it. Needing cheap rubber, he built a factory town modeled on Dearborn in the Amazonian jungle. He sailed a boat around the world in the hopes of convincing Europeans that World War I just wasn't, gosh darn it, *good for business.*

A project even closer to his heart was his utopian fusion of farm and factory life, a new pattern for living by which he hoped, quite literally, to norm the world for all time. This was his famous "Village Industry" concept, in which electric farms, somehow free from animals and fueled by energy from nearby dams, would allow everyone to enjoy the benefits of farm and town life simultaneously.

Ford in some ways represents a return to the New Harmony-like managerial utopianism of the 1840s, an attempt to crack the problem of the future and, by building it here, now, hasten its adoption everywhere. Ford wanted to try this plan in the Upper Peninsula, and, when that didn't pan out, he sketched a thin, long city along the Tennessee River where you'd never be "more than a mile" from the country.

The Fordized farm, of course, simply didn't work—it lowered prices unsustainably and wrecked soil, among other things.

Henry Ford reimagined people as labor-providing robots, solvers of an equation in which the variable for time could be eternally squeezed. He built, in his brain, or in the jungle, an imitation utopia for them, an ersatz Dearborn in which they could never quite make themselves live. He grew old resenting the failure of actual humans to enact a future from which he had quite unconsciously excluded them. Such irrationality could only result, he thought, from Jewish machinations, and he purchased a Dearborn newspaper to disseminate this view.

But his greatest contribution to American racism may not have been *The International Jew* but the affordable car. I wrote above about the disappointment that grips me when I read about the trajectory of the United States between the 1840s and, say, the 1880s. Where did those radical energies go? Those historians who have studied the creation of ghettos offer us at least a partial explanation—and the car is central to it. Kenneth Kusmar, in *A Ghetto Takes Shape* (1978), finds evidence that nineteenth-century Cleveland was *economically* but not *racially* segregated. Poor people tended to live together, but population grew quickly—especially after the completion of the Erie Canal in 1832—and turnover was equally fast. And the vast 1840s influx of anti-slavery New Englanders into Midwestern states turned Cleveland into a comparatively radical city, one where John Brown could live safely and openly for a brief time *after* his famous 1859 raid.

But in the early twentieth century, cities around the country—including Cleveland—remade themselves around the car, and this reshaping, in effect, gave the racists their chance. They took it. Fordism killed the "the walking city of the middle decades of the 19th century," in Kusmar's phrase, "with its haphazard arrangements of stores, businesses, and residential areas," and made possible its replacement by cities with planned neighborhoods. All too often, this meant segregated ones.

Frederick Jackson Turner must have seemed like a kind of prophet at this point. Even the setting in which he gave his paper had an obvious symbolism to it: the annual meeting of the American Historical Association, which the organizers had pushed back by several months so as to coordinate with the Chicago World's Fair. The Fair celebrated the four-hundredth anniversary of Columbus's expedition, and its combination of worldwide scope (delegates and exhibits from everywhere) and national triumphalism staked a clear claim: What Columbus started, Chicago finishes.

Turner's paper makes this subtext text. He starts from the observation that, in the eyes of the government, there is no longer really a "Western frontier." He quotes a report from what we would today call the Census Bureau:

> Up to and including 1880 the country had a frontier of settlement, but at present the unsettled area has been so broken into by isolated bodies of settlement that there can hardly be said to be a frontier line. In the discussion of its extent, its westward movement, etc., it cannot, therefore, any longer have a place in the census reports.

He comments: "This brief official statement marks the closing of a great historical movement." America is settled. There is no more territory for which to light out.

Given what follows, you would expect Turner to find this news depressing. To him, the frontier forced us to be hardy, while "higher social organization" tempered that hardiness, yielding the quintessential American personality: "coarseness and strength combined with acuteness and inquisitiveness." But Turner hedges his bets: "He would be a rash prophet who should assert that the expansive character of American life has now entirely ceased." (Reading this line, you can almost hear Latin America shudder.) He only knows that the country has entered a new phase: "the frontier is gone, and with its going has closed the first period of American history."

So now America is a fully developed, achieved proposition, "Middle" in the sense of "healthfully balanced." We have lived through all our stages of development and come into ourselves at last. The historian Susan Gray detects echoes in Turner's language of then-dominant Lamarckianism: the new characteristics that the "old" races of the world acquired in their struggle to build a world among the prairies and forests would create an actual new, American race, in the pseudo-scientific sense of the term.

As the place equidistant between frontier "coarsensess and strength" and "higher social organization," the Midwest would be, for Turner, the *ne plus ultra* of Americanness. Not coincidentally, in the first part of the twentieth century, writes James Shortridge, "The Middle West came to symbolize the nation . . . to be seen as the most American part of America." Nor is average Americanness the same as average Russianness or average Japaneseness, for the United States has always understood itself, however self-flatteringly, as an experiment on behalf of humanity. Reviewing Turner, Frank Harris wrote:

"[T]he whole world is our nation and simple humanity our countrymen."

Thus, Midwestern averageness, whatever form it may take, has consequences for the entire world; what we make here sets the world's template. And to innovate is to standardize; the new becomes the new normal and then just normal. For a machine to enter mass production, you have to decide on a standard gauge size; for railroads to work, you have to have one kind of spike, one kind of trail; for Flint to be America's future, you have to build an interstate highway system (but not, for example, national passenger rail). A successful innovation, like a utopia, bends the world in its direction. So as the Midwest played host to so many visions of the American future, it also associated itself with the idea of American normality.

Ford and Fordism can be seen as little more than the mass production of averageness: a standard workday, a standard wage, a car that comes in any color as long as it's black. The labor movement, in its negotiations with capital, worked out what many then took as a template for all developed economies. George Gallup was born in Iowa, began his career in Des Moines at Drake University, and worked for a time at Northwestern; Alfred Kinsey scandalized the country from—of all places—Bloomington, Indiana, while Masters and Johnson mapped the female orgasm from St. Louis, a place they had chosen to work because they thought people there were more "normal." Perhaps the Midwest really *is* America's genitals.

Robert and Helen Lynd, setting out in the 1920s to study the "interwoven trends that are the life of a small American city," did not even feel the need to defend the assumption that the chosen city "should, if possible, be in that common-denominator of America, the Middle West." They chose Muncie, Indiana, and called it Middletown. Sinclair Lewis, in *Main Street* and *Babbitt*, associated the Midwest with the vulgarity and acquisitiveness—but also the dull decency and thwarted idealism—that for him defined America. Thorstein Veblen—a Norwegian-American from Wisconsin, and thus, perhaps, a zero degree of Midwesternness—did the same in a series of economics books that read in places a bit like novels, with long, cruel character sketches. Even people who wanted to attack the Midwest couldn't do it without reinforcing this idea. When Van Wyck Brooks decided to attack America as a whole, he did it by conflating it with Midwestern villages and condemning both.

In time, labor militancy led the way to the solution of the problem that neither Fordism nor Progressivism had quite cracked. This was the problem of how to live in the future, to make modern technology, and in particular mass production—which frees us by giving us many cheap and useful goods while imprisoning us with its inflexible routines and demands—our servant rather than our master. (Ford had tried to do this most ambitiously with Village Industry, a quick and quickly notorious failure.) The 1936 Flint General Motors strike—saved, at a key moment, by the refusal of Michigan's New Deal governor, Frank Murphy, to turn the National Guard against the strikers—led to the recognition of the Detroit-based United Auto Workers as a bargaining unit. The success of the strike proved that the recently-passed National Labor Relations Act had teeth, inspired a wave of organizing, and increased the UAW's membership more than tenfold. (A few years later the union even managed to organize Ford, despite Harry Bennett's best efforts.)

From this emerged an uneasy but effective *rapprochement* between labor, management, government, and consumers, a more-or-less coherent, full-fledged economic planning system that became a model for the world. This system even acquired a kind of moral glow, as well, from its role in the Allied victory over the Nazis. Both Ford and the UAW could brag, for example, that they had helped ensure American air power from the Willow Run plant near Ypsilanti; Ford officials and UAW activist Walter Reuther both took on advisory roles in the Roosevelt administration. For all that

Ford was a notorious anti-Semite and intellectual inspiration to Hitler, the humiliation of Nazism was a Ford product—and simultaneously a union-made good. Even when political power returned, at long last, to the Republican Party in the 1950s, nobody really wanted to disturb this arrangement too much. By midcentury, the era's greatest economist—John Kenneth Galbraith, in *The New Industrial State* (1967)—could write about this system as a thing that, with timely and careful tweaks administered by a caste of technocrats, might function indefinitely. 1950s Flint was everyone's future.

The British journalist David Graham Hutton, in his 1946 *Midwest at Noon*, surveys a world of Midwestern exemplarity triumphant. Traveling through the region, he meets "businessmen, mechanics, Mexicans of the Southwest, newspapermen, Negroes, cops [leave it to a white British guy to list these side-by-side], sheriffs, farmers, lawyers, welders, and very many children." And he thinks we are just swell: "courteous, congenial, friendly, and diverting," he writes in one place; "realistic, matter-of-fact, self-critical, and adaptable" in another. "There has not been one unpleasant experience in my journeyings," he tells us, like a Minnesota bourgeois.

The Midwest fascinates Hutton in its seeming exemption from history. Early in the book, he wonders why Midwesterners haven't, on the one hand, succumbed to the violent political enthusiasms that spread across Europe in the thirties, and why, on the other hand, so many Midwesterners in particular were slow to enter European conflicts such as the one he came here to sell us. The theory he comes up with is that the "extremes and violent challenges" of the region—bad weather, temperamental soil, Indians (who don't count as Midwesterners)—leave us too drained to join the Blackshirts. "The male virtues, and devices, can be used to their utmost there without any effort to find ways of doing it," he writes. The contemporary reader might want to ask Hutton a few questions: *Why do you take European history as a template from which Midwesterners have somehow deviated? And what do you mean, "male" devices? That was a gag gift.*

But his point is clear: our bad weather has shaped us, has alternately toughened and smoothed us for a special role in the human future. (If we have no history, the future is the only time to which we can belong.) Circumstance has prepared us to settle the conflict that will define the future of the human race: that between "standardization and conformity," as represented on the one hand by large, stable business concerns, powerful unions, and interventionist New Deal policies; and on the other hand by individualism, the obsessiveness-verging-on-crankery of Edison or Ford or Kellogg. He hopes that from this conflict, the Midwest's "initiative, enterprise, vigor, and curiosity" will "produce a new type of individual." "Naturally," he concludes, "it is on this favored nation, and on the most favorite in the most American region in it, that so many anxious eyes are fixed." He concludes that "there is something of destiny" in its triumph.

In this last phrase he seems to draw on another, slightly older strain of commentary on the Midwest: the utopian, prophetic style. In its earliest manifestations, this sort of talk is indistinguishable from advertising. The historian R.C. Buley—who positively reviewed Hutton's book, and whose Pulitzer-winning 1950 book *The Old Northwest Pioneer Period* was the flagship for a brief postwar efflorescence in Midwestern historiography—quotes a "legislator in Missouri Territory" who wrote, in 1816:

Looking only a few years through the vista of futurity, what a sublime spectacle presents itself! Wilderness, once the chosen residence of solitude or savageness, converted into populous cities, smiling villages, beautiful farms and plantations! The happy multitude, busy in their daily occupations, manifests contentment and peace, breathing their gratitude and prayers only to the great King of Kings! The wild Indian, taught by mild persuasion and example is become an enthusiast in the cause of civilization . . . What a scene—how beautiful, how grand!—yet not ideal: another century will realize it. Yes—this fine country is destined to become the finest foothold of the Genius of American Liberty.

What this forgotten writer announced as prophecy, Hutton catalogued as settled fact. Here, at last, in the Midwest, humanity could arrive. For Turner, the Midwest had served as the place where America's present met and somewhat civilized its future; for Hutton, the Midwest plays that role not only for a country, but for the entire human species. The whole world was the nation, simple humanity our countrymen.

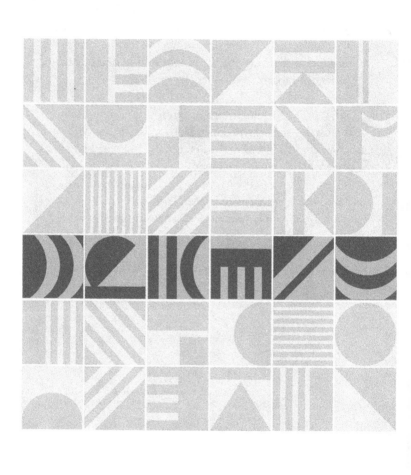

ROW 4

NORMALITY AND ITS DISCONTENTS

Midwestern literature—and literature written by non-Midwesterners about the region—has long played with tropes of normality, averageness, unpretentiousness. Superman may be an alien, but Clark Kent came from Kansas—the home that there is no place like *because* it's anyplace. John Hughes's everykid protagonists—his breakfast clubbers, privileged truants, and lip-biting Molly Ringwald heroines—all came from Illinois. When John Ford wanted to stress Lincoln's everyman qualities, he made *Abe Lincoln in Illinois*. When John Carpenter wanted to make a film of schematic purity, banality meeting pure evil, he trucked in dead leaves, scattered them on California streets, called the town Haddonfield, Illinois, and titled his movie *Halloween* as though it were a generic product you'd buy at Kroger.

The first novel written by a Michigander, a book published only three years after statehood, already hints at this idea of the Midwest as an evened-out, smoothed-to-perfection place, precisely balanced between wildness and civilization. "'Tis true there are but meagre materials for anything which might be called a story," writes Caroline Kirkland in *A New Home— Who'll Follow?* (1841). "I have never seen a cougar—nor been bitten by a rattlesnake. The reader who has patience to go with me . . . must expect nothing beyond a meandering recital of commonplace occurrences." She also promises "mere gossip about everyday people" and "a very ordinary pen-drawing." *Oh, it's nothing big. Oh, we're nothing special.* (It's hilarious to me that white Midwesterners already sounded this way when we lived in mudholes and feared Native attack at any moment.)

But the political purport of this aw-shucks-we're-just-plain-folks modesty becomes clear just a few pages into the book, where Kirkland writes:

> A home on the outskirts of civilization—habits of society which allow the maid and her mistress to do the honors in complete equality, and to make the social tea visit in loving conjunction—such a distribution of the duties of life as compels all, without distinction, to rise with the sun or before him—to breakfast with the chickens, then "count the slow clock and dine exactly at noon"—to be ready for tea at four, and for bed at eight—may certainly be expected to furnish some curious particulars for the consideration of those whose daily course almost reverses this primitive arrangement.

We don't dump *everything* on our servants, like *you* people. *We* don't have *slaves*, like prissy Southerners. *We* don't put on airs. It's a power move familiar to every Midwesterner.

The idea of Midwesterners as normal underlies the idea of Midwesterners as egalitarians. If you read books about Midwestern history, you'll encounter the two words together almost incessantly. If, however, we take "egalitarianism" as an idea that is meant to cover all actually existing people—and I take this to be the only meaningful form of egalitarianism—it fails as a description of Midwestern political history. (Not that there are many places it *does* describe.)

Think of humble, unpretentious Indiana, the place John Mellencamp was thinking of when he sang of the virtues of small towns. Back in the twenties, Indiana was the center of the Klan revival. Klansmen thought—and still think—of the capacity for self-rule as a racial inheritance, something like a cask of presumably excellent wine handed down undrunk from generation to generation. If you let Catholics or black people have it, you're not just wasting it; you're actually destroying what little democracy there is, ensuring there will be none left for those of us whose genetic and cultural inheritance will allow them, at some undetermined point in the future, to enjoy it. ("Look what Jim Crow's done and gone / Went and changed his name / Don't know what he's going by these days / But he's still actin' the same," John Mellencamp also sang—for his egalitarianism is real, and at times so awkwardly sincere that it's hard to look at.)

Similar beliefs inspired the activities of those white Detroiters who fought for restrictive housing covenants. In some cases, those beliefs—perhaps not spelled out with the same explicitness—inspired the inactivity of those white Detroiters who failed to fight against their racist neighbors. And of course, in every city where this process played itself out, many white people were simply apathetic, or ignorant, or overwhelmed by their own lives—for life is nothing if not overwhelming. If American history proves anything, it is that a core of committed racists will always beat a large crowd of noncommittal non-racists. Since, in a capitalist economy, land is a family's ultimate security—both a home that you can always retreat to and a fund you can always spend—an organized conspiracy to lower the value of black-owned land gives the whole game away. You can't call a place where this happens "egalitarian."

Thus, while Southern history yields story after story of the most savage, intimate racist violence—of men castrated and barbecued before smiling crowds dressed for a picnic—Midwestern history is a study in racial quarantine, enforced by banks, real estate sales, neighborhood covenants, city councils, and police. The lack of the physical barriers between populations that are built into Southern cities—the road that abruptly cuts off; the abrupt strip of woods between neighborhoods—just makes the absurdity of the social barriers more visible. And though the region has seen its share of Klan activity and outright lynchings—Chicago's Red Summer in 1919 is as ugly a moment as American history affords—Midwestern racism most frequently appears in the history books in the form of riots: Detroit, 1943; Cleveland, 1966; Milwaukee, Cincinnati, and Detroit again, 1967; Chicago, Cincinnati again, and Kansas City, 1968; Detroit again, 1975; Cincinnati again, 2001; Ferguson, 2014; Milwaukee again, 2016. A riot is, among other things, a refusal to be quarantined. We like to tell a story in which "white flight" responds to late-sixties uprisings, a choice that makes such flight seem, at least, rational. (Those who can afford to tend to remove themselves from physical danger; this is not necessarily culpable.) But the riots themselves arose from already-ongoing abuse.

Egalitarianism is a process, not an achievement. When it becomes something for a region to pride itself upon, it is probably lost.

The Midwest quarantines its other nonwhite populations, too—the people from Mexico and further south, from the hills of Laos or the highlands of Somalia, from the Middle East, who commute from their neighborhoods to city centers or suburban farms, to harvest grain, empty bedpans, and drive snowplows. We do it with residential segregation and gentrification.

We do it, too, with rumors, with convenient vaguenesses, with myth. When what is normal fails, it looks to the margins to explain its failure. When Ford's projects began to falter, when he encountered resistance he couldn't beat, he suddenly discovered, as though it were a new-built facility of yet-unstated purpose that had suddenly opened up in his heart, a hatred for Jews.

Reading Sujey Vega's ethnography of Latinos in Indiana, *Latino Heartland* (2014), I encountered this charming anecdote:

> . . . a running narrative throughout the town placed sole responsibility [for a surge in undocumented immigration] on one employer rumored to have placed a billboard on the U.S.-Mexican border to entice undocumented immigrants to Lafayette. This story was related to me on multiple occasions when I spoke to White residents about their knowledge of the immigrant population. Further investigation of this anecdote revealed that contrary to popular opinion, news of any such billboard was never reported in the newspaper. In fact, upon contacting the business beat reporter often associated with this story, I was told, "That may be an urban legend."

Specificity accosts people; it surmounts our little credibility tests. If you ask a person if they have any spare change, they'll say no; if you ask them for forty-seven cents, exactly, they'll fish in their pocket without thinking. Similarly, perhaps, if you said, to the white people of Lafayette, Indiana, "Illegal Mexicans are coming here to make their lives better!" at least some would shrug. But if you introduce a specific, odd, and fictitious billboard into the discourse, they'll react to that, and the ground of argument shifts.

Thomas Sugrue's classic study of Detroit, *The Origins of the Urban Crisis* (1996), reports that during the 1940s, many white people believed that black people had formed a conspiracy—a "bump club"—to intentionally jostle them in the street. I first encountered this detail soon after the mid-2010s moral panic regarding the "knockout game," in which national media accused black people of playing a game in which they bum-rushed white passersby for fun. (The "game" existed, but was neither common nor clearly racial; white kids did it too.)

And speaking of apocrypha: no professional disappointment on my part has ever failed to result in a denunciation, by some friend or relative, of a certain wheelchair-bound black lesbian, a woman who, it seems, has nothing better to do but roll around from one job or graduate program to another, stealing *my* spot. (My state banned affirmative action in 2006, at least a century too soon.) I keep saying she, like Midwestern egalitarianism, is mythical, but nobody believes me.

When I try to imagine what it must be like to contend with such an atmosphere of rumor, I think of an encounter at the beginning of Ida B. Wells's history of the 1917 race riots in East St. Louis, Illinois. She has already ignored the "advice of both the Pullman and the train conductors" in going there at all, reasoning that the state's governor has already passed through:

> No one molested me in my walk from the station to the City Hall, although I did not see a single colored person until I reached the City Hall building. I accosted the lone individual in soldier's uniform at the depot, a mere boy with a gun, and asked him if the governor was in town. When he said no, he had gone to Washington the night before, I asked how the situation was and he said, "bad." I asked what was the trouble and he said, "The Negroes won't let the whites alone. They killed seven yesterday and three already this morning." It was only 7 o'clock in the

morning and I decided he was lying, so said nothing more on that score.

Of course the soldier is lying. He may or may not know it. Notice his pronouns: *The Negroes won't let the whites alone. They killed seven yesterday.* Who is "they"? The previous sentence mentions both black and white people. What the second sentence tells us is that, in a generalized way, *there is violence*, with both agent and target unclear. The "Negroes" of the first sentence are guilty by parataxis. In a psychological sense, the soldier is telling a truth about the way white people experience the violence that (other) whites, generally speaking, initiate. Whoever shot first, *They* did it, simply by being around, being loud, making demands, playing music, taking jobs. But the vagueness of the pronoun also allows him to distance himself from his own racism.

The soldier in this anecdote could be my classmate, my neighbor, my cousin—could be me, up to around age seventeen. If you were black, and you accompanied me, back then, to some social function in the places where I grew up or went to college—a wedding, say—we'd welcome you with open arms. Even my most conservative friends or relatives would treat you with far more warmth and respect than you'd get from some Boomer-age professional-class white liberal Democrats. We'd like you so much that, by the end of the conversation, we'd be looking out for you. How long are you in town for? Better stay away from this or that neighborhood. Are you going through Chicago? Listen—and here we'd lean in close, confidential, as though about to share a trick for saving on your income tax—if someone flashes their brights at you, *don't flash back.* That's how the gangs decide who to shoot. Yes, we'll say, mistaking the meaning of your widening eyes, your dismayed mouth, it's terrible what they do.

I would not begin to know how to make my way among such people—and I *am* such people.

In Toni Morrison's *Song of Solomon* (1977), one of the great Midwestern novels, Michigan is a compromise location for a black family that may have an untapped ability to fly back to Africa, or beyond to some place none of us yet know. It's not a place of safety; it's just *somewhat better*. This is the sense one receives from reading the testimony of those who moved north during the Great Migration. There's the feeling of a stalled movement, a kind of midwayness about this treacherous place. You might think you're safe there, but Michigan's prison system is as racist, Minneapolis's police department as brutal, as anywhere in the country. These are compromise locations, halfway to acceptable.

Writing more recently, Vanessa Taylor suggests that the region's tropes don't quite fit African Americans: "Within this imagined landscape of white blue-collar life, there's the dismissal of Black people that shaped Midwestern cultures. Cities with rich Black culture and history, like Chicago and St. Louis, get pushed into their own class." Roxane Gay writes of a place that alternates between seeing her as "curiosity" or "threat," seemingly at whim.

Tanisha C. Ford relates the story of traveling through Martinsville, Indiana, in the late eighties, and watching her mother and aunt argue over whether to stop in that former Klan "epicenter" when the car's headlights break.

No one in our car uttered the words "sundown town"; that was a language I'd come to know later in life. For now, I was getting a particular kind of geography lesson. I didn't know where Martinsville was on a map in relationship to Fort Wayne, but I was learning that I wasn't supposed to be there.

How exhausting, though in a way mentally strengthening, to have to maintain a second map in the mind—the Indiana white people see, and the Indiana that might kill you. How tiring, though educational, to be forced to read white faces and decipher white silences.

The racism of the Midwest is, in part, a fulfillment of the violence inherent in the idea of "settling" what was already occupied. We're still settling. Think of those people who move to Detroit, start a coffee shop, become (even more) comfortably upper-middle-class, and sigh, "Just a few years ago there was *nothing* here!" The writer Lyz Lenz, in her memoir *God Land* (2019), calls this sort of thing, correctly, a "colonizing impulse": to look somewhere and "see a barren landscape that needs your new ideas." Even long-settled cities become a fund that must be made to pay.

But the racism of the region is also a terrible betrayal of what is best in its history and its present. The Movement For Black Lives is a partly Midwestern creation—it began with Ferguson, Missouri, grew at a Cleveland conference, shut down a Minnesota airport. The resistance he met in Michigan was one of the reasons that the white supremacist Richard Spencer ended his speaking tour and, to an extent, his public career. Today ICE struggles to find a Midwestern city that will let it build a concentration camp. Midwestern antiracist and antifascist groups are making that happen.

In Marilynne Robinson's *Gilead* (2004)—another great Midwestern novel—John Ames, a descendant of Iowa abolitionists, compares his once-radical, now-staid hometown to an ember upon which God once breathed and "turn[ed] to radiance." But his godson and namesake, John Ames Boughton—a ne'er-do-well whose best trait is his loyalty to a secret black girlfriend and child—visits this Gilead, hoping to find a place of refuge for his family. He reminds Ames of another smoldering thing:

But then he said, "What about this town? If we came here and got married, could we live here? Would people leave us alone?"

Well, I didn't know the answer to that one, either. I thought so.

He said, "There was a fire at the Negro church."

"That was a little nuisance fire, and it happened many years ago."

"And it has been many years since there was a Negro church."

Of course there wasn't much I could say to that.

In the novel Ames often speaks of the "humility" of the town. The trilogy (thus far) of novels to which *Gilead* belongs has restored, for many readers, a sense of the radical sweep of early Midwestern history, but the books are, in their way, deeply humiliating as well, both because they illustrate the compromises and failures that followed that moment—even lovable Ames can't quite admit here what the reader is forced to see—and because they reveal to us our silliness in condescending to the Midwest.

To be "humiliated," of course, is good. It is a profoundly democratic exercise to remember that you are humus, the organic part of soil; that you are temporarily excited ground. That you are intent dirt. Wendell Berry writes that soil is Christlike "in its passivity and beneficence, and in the penetrating energy that issues out of its peaceableness. . . . It keeps the past, not as history or as memory, but as richness, new possibility." To have a history is to be made of many alive wriggling moldy embarrassments that preexisted you and over which you have no control. To live inside history is to be forced to tack back and forth between the *I* of personal experience and the *you* who emerges from and lives in history and place—this weird double who shares one's name but who is bounded and predictable, hagridden by traits and habits, as the open *I* never is. There *I* had been, an open eye wandering the world, a congress of not-quite-articulated desires and impulses clinging together to that single letter *I* as to a piece of driftwood in the open sea; and suddenly there was *he*, with his mother's verbal tics and his father's knuckles, a stolid third-person bound from dust to dust.

Perhaps in the idea of soil, in humility, is an image of what is normal that is broad enough to include everybody, as the soil itself one day will.

The idea of normalcy can give safety, warmth, the smugness of a person whose plate is full. It can make us feel invulnerable, passed-over by history and its dangers. "Basic personhood" seems too broad for the grave, like something that would survive even Biblical conflagration; or nuclear war; or the predictable, obvious, long-foretold consequences of a carbon economy.

But it can also be, even for those it is meant to cover, far more trouble than it's worth. There is something deeply unsettling to us in the idea that we have arrived; it provokes anxiety, a sense that one is not yet fit somehow.

"Again, I think it would be somewhat different if it wasn't for the wind," says the narrator of Oscar Micheaux's 1913 novel *The Conquest*. He has, he tells us, left home to farm in South Dakota, where the wind "blows and blows until it makes me feel lonesome and so far away from that little place and the country in southern Illinois." And then, seemingly unconscious of the contradiction, he narrates all the reasons he never felt at home there either, or in Minneapolis, where his family moves in his teens. In our terms, the novel is nearly autofiction—the narrator tells us that his name is Devereaux, then, teasingly, that this "is not my name but we will call it that for this sketch." Lest we miss the point, he adds, "It is a peculiar name that ends with an 'eaux.'" And the plot of the novel closely follows the story of Micheaux's years as a South Dakota homesteader, his unsuccessful early marriage, with minor variations—Devereaux heads to Minneapolis when Micheaux headed to Chicago, for example.

Even telling his own story, Micheaux—who having homesteaded in the Midwest went on to be another kind of pioneer, as one of the first black movie directors—has to create a kind of double, who *almost* makes his decisions, *almost* lives his life. On the first page, he quotes a poem, "Opportunity," that someone handed him years ago—"I've a notion to burn it," the narrator says wryly. It's the kind of encouraging doggerel that working people of all kinds have tacked onto living room walls and cabinet doors from time immemorial, but juxtaposed against that South Dakota "wind" and loneliness, it sounds uncanny:

Master of human destinies am I.
Fame, love, and fortune on my footsteps wait.
Cities and fields I walk. I penetrate
Deserts and seas remote, and passing by
Hovel, and mart, and palace—soon or late
I knock unbidden once at every gate.
If sleeping, wake—if feasting, rise before
I turn away.

Opportunity itself travels the landscape as a kind of fugitive, a transient. You stay awake nights watching for it as though it were the hostile stranger who will kill you.

The Midwest seems to offer us the chance to become normal, but what this means in practice is a paranoid sense that you've missed it, were five degrees off, that your chance came to town, missed you, and jumped on a train, vowing that it will not be here again. You are shadowed by people so like you they might as well be you. Perhaps you are the imposter, the double they cannot claim.

A person who is told that they are normal might adopt a posture of vigilant defense, both internal and external, against anything that might weaken their claim to the label. Any emotion spiky or passionate enough to disrupt the smooth surface of normality must be shunted away. Garrison Keillor and David Letterman made careers from talking about this repression in a comic mode that both embodies it and transmutes it into art. The Minnesota writer Carol Bly finds it less amusing:

> [In the Midwest] there is a restraint against *feeling in general.* There is a restraint against enthusiasm ("real nice" is the adjective—not "marvelous"); there is restraint in grief ("real sober" instead of "heartbroken"); and always, always, restraint in showing your feelings, lest someone be drawn closer to you. ... When someone has stolen all four wheels off your car you say, "Oh, when I saw that car, with the wheels stripped off like that, I just thought ohhhhhhhh."

Critiques of emotional repression always risk imposing a single model for the Healthy Expression of Emotions on a healthy range of variations. But anyone who has lived in the Midwest will recognize the behavior Bly describes. At worst it can lead to a kind of self-doubling. David Rhodes's *The Last Fair Deal Going Down* (1972) posits a terrifying hidden cannibal city underneath Des Moines, consisting of those people who cannot make themselves live aboveground lives. It is a powerful image of emotional repression, though it owes some of its power, as great literary images always do, to the fact that it cannot be wholly reduced to a stand-in for something else.

Midwestern literature, as I've said, has given us some of our classic images of normality; it has also borne witness to a sense of loneliness unique in American literature, a sense of impermanence on the landscape, of a fragile hold on the place that you call home, or an uncanny sense of a second, nonstandard self, a terrifying ghost who is also you. Think of the man in Sherwood Anderson's *Winesburg, Ohio*, who writes his thoughts on scraps of paper and then throws them at the ground. Think of Cather's Jim, in *My Ántonia*, who lives his adulthood pressed under a love he can't quite allow to realize itself. Or Evan S. Connell's *Mrs. Bridge*, calling from her garage to no one. Of Toni Morrison's *Sula*, whose singularity isolates her even as it makes of her a kind of hero. Of Richard Wright's Cross Damon, in *The Outsider,* choosing to live as a kind of ghost of himself after a mistaken report of his own death liberates him from the boredom of having an identity. Of the heroines of Dawn Powell's early novels, waiting for something unnameable. Of every word William H. Gass wrote.

Horror and science fiction, in particular, have made much of the Midwest, often using it as an image of everyday normality that hides a series of evil doubles or stands upon a shadow world of nasty impulses. Elm Street, that bland place where nightmare threatens to overtake reality, is somewhere in Ohio. In Robert Heinlein's 1951 novel *The Puppet Masters*, body-snatching alien "slugs" mount their world takeover from Des Moines, as though aiming at humanity's dead center. Thomas Disch's *Camp Concentration* (1969) posits a future Iowa where Vietnam War dissenters are imprisoned in a vast camp, given an experimental form of syphilis, and turned into doomed geniuses who will be used as a brain trust. In other works Disch gives us vampires in the Twin Cities, a Minneapolis haunted by ghosts and witches and demon children, and an

Iowa, again, where the local government has made it illegal for flying mutants to fly.

In the 2014 film *It Follows*, an unstoppable, sexually-transmitted curse, figured as a slow-walking but indomitable monster, follows a teenage girl after she loses her virginity to a boy. She and her group of friends, living on the edge of post-industrial Detroit, try a series of strategems to destroy the thing; a disturbing, underplayed scene toward the end suggests that they resort, in desperation, to the exploitation of black, marginalized sex workers who live inside the city. They don't set out to be racist; but when you live in a structure, and the walls of the structure close in . . .

More recently, the 2018 graphic novel *Middlewest*, by Skottie Young and Jorge Corona, concerns an abused boy who lives in a kind of interior America rendered fantastic as much by its adherence to nostalgic tropes (A paper route? A fun fair?) as by its talking fox and its tornado monster. The beloved television show *Stranger Things* (2017–) achieves a similar effect in its use of Indiana.

True crime and noir have played with the Midwestern setting as well, to memorable effect: *Bonnie and Clyde* (1967); *In Cold Blood* (1965); *Badlands* (1974); *The Honeymoon Killers* (1970); the novels of Tom Drury. Stephen Graham Jones's *The Bird Has Gone* (2003) sets its central murder mystery in a future Great Plains region returned, by treaty, to Native Americans.

In our own time, probably no artist has explored these tropes more deeply than David Lynch—a filmmaker whose best works seem to be all these genres simultaneously. It may seem perverse to claim him for the Midwest, in that he grew up in Montana. This is part of what makes his exploration so potent; he takes up stories that are *nearly* Midwestern, such as the Pittsburgh/Rust Belt setting of *Eraserhead*. *Twin Peaks* uses the Pacific Northwest setting as well as any work of art ever has. *Twin Peaks* was also originally called, and set in, North

Dakota. An important subplot of its third season takes place, in fact, in South Dakota.

Blue Velvet—which I always remember as taking place in Iowa even though it's actually North Carolina—represents yet another version of a classic American literary trope: the decent, clean town in which I live contains a dark underbelly, and I must fix my loyalty to one side or the other, for I have pieces of both within me. (As many have pointed out, it is "Young Goodman Brown" redone as noir.) Its hero, Jeffrey Beaumont, is repelled but also fascinated by the villainous Frank, and falls in love with Frank's girlfriend/victim, Dorothy, who represents both the town's seedy underworld and Jeffrey's less creditable sexual desires.

The film realizes Jeffrey's struggle with such potency that its moral dualism begins to seem shallow only in retrospect—in comparison to *Twin Peaks*. The latter sets up a conflict similar to that of *Blue Velvet*—a nice town to raise kids in, secretly riven by incest and cocaine and underage prostitution and demon possession, all of it linked, in some unstated way, with the presence—and perhaps with the genocide?—of Native Americans. Had Lynch followed through on his original plan to set the show in North Dakota, it would have had a drastically different look and feel—none of those "fantastic trees" that our hero, Agent Cooper, so admires—but most of the themes would have continued to work. It is easy to imagine a North Dakota town standing in for decent normality.

But while *Blue Velvet* sets up a dualistic struggle and asks "Which will triumph?" or "Which is realest?" *Twin Peaks* creates a series of doubles that have total autonomy, neither of which unambiguously wins. The profoundly decent Agent Cooper, the cutely idiotic Dougie Jones, and the terrifying Mr. C—the three faces of white American male authority—are all equally real, and none ever achieves a final triumph over the other; in our final glimpse of Cooper, as he stands utterly lost on the sidewalk in front of what he thought was Laura Palmer's home but is in reality yet another malevolent pocket universe, he seems to bear traces of all of them. All along, they display similarities to each other—Dougie's long-suffering wife, encountering Agent Cooper in the person of her husband, looks at him as though he both transcends and somehow completes whatever she once loved in Dougie. Cooper's determination to solve every case can shade off into a Machiavellianism that reminds us of Mr. C.

And this is the unbearable truth of the Midwest, of America. The picture-postcard city where neighbors pitch in during a storm and the sundown town are the same place. The Minneapolis that welcomes immigrants and the Minneapolis that allows its police to beat the poor are the same place. The Michigan that helped beat the Confederacy and the Michigan where white people lock their car doors while drifting through Saginaw are the same place. One does not disprove the other. One is not the underbelly of the other. One will not finally triumph over the other. We have to reckon with both simultaneously; or we must admit to *being* both simultaneously.

For, obviously, no one is just *normal*. A species is a bounded set of variations on a template, not an achieved state of being. A person is many things at once. (Imagine an *average* patch of soil. Both people and dirt are defined by heterogeneity at every level.)

To tell someone they're normal is to make them neurotic. If that neurosis takes none of the other forms I've described, it takes this one: an intense alienation and disgust, which a person might project inward—*What is wrong with me?*—or outward, in a kind of bomb-the-suburbs reflex.

I took the first option. As a child, I felt that I came from nowhere too definite. If I saw Michigan acknowledged in print anywhere—aside from Detroit, our agreed-upon Important City—I started as though I had encountered my own double. In science class, when I learned that the next town over, St. Louis, had made headlines in the late '70s as the spot of a famous industrial accident—someone mixed up cattle feed with a carcinogenic flame retardant, thus poisoning land, food, bodily fat, breast milk, and, to at least some small degree, six in ten Michiganders, down to today—I felt vertigo. How could history have happened where I live?

Since I was a Human in a Place, without further specification, I assumed too that my town contained within it every possible human type. If I could not fit in here, I would not fit in anywhere. ("Fitting in" I defined as being occupied on Friday nights and, sooner or later, kissing a girl.) Every week that passed in which I did not meet these criteria—which was basically all of them—became a prophecy. Every perception, every idea, every opinion that I could not make immediately legible to my peers became proof of an almost metaphysical estrangement, an oceanic differentness that could not be changed and could not be borne. I would obsessively examine tiny failures of communication for days, always blaming myself. It never occurred to me that this problem might be accidental or temporary. I knew that cities existed, but they were all surely just Michigan farm towns joined together n number of times, depending on population. Owing to a basically phlegmatic temperament, and the fear of hurting my parents, I made it to college without committing suicide. I'm fine now, but it wasn't fun getting there. I wouldn't wish those years on other people.

Mine was, perhaps, an advanced case of the vertigo normalcy induces. A much more common malady is the truly bizarre self-alienation that I encounter among so many straight, white Midwesterners I meet—a strong conviction that their own experiences are too banal for examination or even, sometimes, description. Or there's the self-contempt that imitates, but prevents, genuine self-scrutiny and self-criticism while creating a misery far worse (if for no other reason than that it's unending) than what comes from a frank acceptance of one's failures and a square resolve to do better. You find this often among young white Midwesterners who lean left. They hate themselves, not just performatively. They view themselves with the kind of self-contempt that precludes genuine self-criticism. They say, "Ugh, I'm the *worst*," or, "I can't wait for the Revolution to kill me" rather than "I shouldn't have skipped that demonstration." They do this, at least, for as long as they're psychologically able—which isn't long. They grow out of it; or, perhaps, they give up on activism, blaming it for their misery.

Among people who are relatively apolitical—that is, among people who lean toward the right and don't know it—one often finds that sense of having missed something, having blown a chance, that I've described above. In both cases, it makes people feel that they're boring, even as they seethe at the failure of those around them to acknowledge their roiling depths. It makes them timid or conformist. It drives them to check their car models, their lawns, their affect against the neighbors, or against the people they have convinced themselves their neighbors are. It gaslights them into never really looking at those neighbors; surely they are as dull as we fear we might be.

Among artsy people, it can lead to the feeling—false almost by definition, and ubiquitous among white, relatively-not-poor Midwestern artsy kids—that nothing has ever happened to you. There was, a few years ago, a television show—one so over-discussed I cannot type its name without nausea—that came close to dealing with this dilemma in a thoughtful way. Its hero, a college graduate from East Lansing, Michigan, wanted to write books and conquer New York, but she so disbelieved that anything story-worthy had ever happened in her life that she exploited the experiences of others just so that she could do her work. In one particularly disturbing episode, she lured a recovering addict—who she knew was attracted to her—into buying crack for her, so that she could "have an experience" that would enable her to write. At the end of that season, she spiraled into a total collapse—which ought to have struck her as some sort of purchase, at least, on being interesting. (Then the show failed to resolve this interesting and, to me, extremely believable plotline, returning to its initial mode of adapting to film its showrunner/star's self-flattering daydreams, whereupon I stopped watching.)

The Midwest became central to so many of this country's stories about itself in part because some of it is naturally rich, productive. But that is not a normal thing to be; it is precisely a gift, something generous and prodigious. That we take such a good place for granted, as though its usefulness for human life were proof of its dullness and interchangeability, allows us to misuse it, and ourselves, and each other, who are marked as boring by having come from this boringly good thing, or marked as threatening because they didn't. It takes a thousand years for the earth to make three centimeters of topsoil. (Climate change encourages floods, which wash topsoil out to sea.)

ROW 5

MIDWEST AT MIDNIGHT

I f Hutton imagined a Midwest just reaching high noon, more recent writers use a tone that varies between chastened and scared. If the Midwesterner of the early twentieth century represented an America coming into its own, the Midwesterner of the twenty-first symbolizes a center failing to hold. If "anxious eyes" are still fixed here, it is to survey a representative unease.

"To live here," writes Meghan O'Gieblyn, "is to develop a wariness of all forms of unqualified optimism." Thomas Frank alludes to "The wreckage that you see every day as you tour this part of the country." In an excellent piece on voter suppression in Kansas, Sarah Smarsh invokes the old the-Midwest-*is*-the-country language only to invert it, to make of it a warning: "Whatever is the matter with Kansas is the matter with Washington, too." Fiction writers long ago discovered veins of noir and gothic in the region's burned-out cities and meth-hardened countrysides. Even in dire straits, the Midwest is still America's future and bellwether.

What happened? At this point it is commonplace to invoke "the death of the Midwestern manufacturing base," and to mention, with a sigh, Detroit or Gary or Youngstown. "Death" is already a misnomer. Not all the factories have closed, nor is there any reason to assume that practices such as offshoring, say, can continue indefinitely at present rates. To say "death" is to impose a teleology on a process that may not be going anywhere in particular.

A reader who tries to figure out when exactly this death began—who stabbed whom, or who fell, or who was pushed— will encounter great obfuscation, as is always true of someone who sets out to understand economic history. (It turns out to be a very interesting subject that, in the popular press, is shorn of just enough context to make it impenetrable.) Challenges to the postwar economic arrangement, with possible bad implications for Midwesterners, were already clear to some as early as 1961. In a pamphlet from that year, Solomon Barkin wrote:

> Another disturbing trend has been the shift in industrial location from the East and the Middle West, where unions have been strong, to the South and to smaller communities where unions still have limited influence. Bargaining rights do not move with the plant.

After the Taft-Hartley Act of 1947, which responded to a wave of postwar strikes by allowing states to pass anti-union "right-to-work" laws—laws that those who live under them aptly describe as "the right to work for less"—a number of Southern states did accordingly. Absent legal coercion or an unusual degree of conscientiousness, an employer will tend to choose a situation that offers them the most power over employees. Accordingly, many companies looking to open new plants during the '50s and '60s sited them in the Sun Belt rather than in the Midwest. Decades later, companies would use Mexico in the same way.

The oil supply shocks of the 1970s, meanwhile, weakened the political power of the manufacturing sector and strengthened energy. A 1980 *New York Times* story summarizes the country's direction by contrasting new skyscrapers in Houston against a shuttered bar in Detroit. The government's inability to find a simple fix for the energy problem seemed to demonstrate the limits of the entire post-New Deal order. (This was the case even though the problem itself—an oil embargo imposed by OPEC states cooperating internationally, in retaliation for U.S. support of Israel during the Yom Kippur War—was also, in its way, a demonstration of the power of central planning.) In *The Reckoning*, his 1986 comparative study of the American and Japanese auto industries, David Halberstam writes:

> Now, in the erosion of the great American industrial core, the workers if not the managers had an intuitive sense that there was something indelible about the decline, and that the region would never again be what it had been, so by 1982 a new migration was well underway. It was sending hundreds of thousands of Americans, white and black, from the Great Lakes region to the booming, energy-dominated economy of the Southwest. For although the skyrocketing of energy prices had helped undermine the industrial base of America, it had made the business of oil and all its byproduct industries suddenly more successful than ever.

He goes on to describe a Detroit in which a jobless man stayed solvent by driving to Houston on the weekends and returning with a truck full of the city's Sunday papers, then selling those papers at a premium to people who wanted to study the want ads.

Some writers present the shift away from manufacturing in the late twentieth century (a somewhat better phrase than "death," or the best I could do on a deadline) as a moral tale. The big midcentury firms let themselves get *too* successful; a good time, too long continued, left them unprepared to deal with misfortune. The "misfortune" varies depending on who's telling the tale, though it often comes from the East. In the 1980s, there were the lean, efficient Japanese companies that made lean, efficient vehicles, like Toyota. In the 1990s, there were the cheap goods made by the four countries—South Korea, Singapore, Taiwan, and Hong Kong—to which the business press applied the quaintly racist label "Asian Tigers." More recently, there is the so-called "rise of China," which is responsible for most of the 2000s' much-touted reduction in extreme poverty.

In its most reactionary form, this story often just castigates "unions"—workers—for wishing to live well, for being other than perfect victims. Ford and GM employees forced the companies to pay them too well, to give them pensions no one could possibly deserve, and this left these poor corporations with no alternative but to move their operations to Sun Belt cities, and then to Mexico. It is always amusing, among other things, to hear this argument from well-paid employees of Washington thinktanks, who often make more than union wages merely for being willing to hold the kinds of opinions a person has to be *paid* to hold.

Such explanations for the "death," or "decline," or perhaps simply—who yet knows?—the "long pause," in the history of Midwestern manufacturing ultimately suffer from the incoherence that afflicts victim-blaming in any form. They remind me of the arguments of Thomas Malthus, who bid the poor starve now so that they wouldn't have to do so later. If misfortune was always bound to return in some form—as, in this veil of tears, it probably is—why berate people for snatching a few decades of relative happiness before it does so?

The argument that manufacturing firms themselves were at fault for the shift has somewhat more force when it targets those who, in effect, were driving the car at the time. At most firms, this probably did not include workers, whom it was common to exclude from discussions about quality control by contract. This was a concession demanded by management. One union-worker's-son-turned-economist recalls that his father, who had festooned the shop floor with signs declaring "Quality is Our Concern Too!" got besieged with angry phone calls from management who reminded him, citing his own contract, that it wasn't.

It is also possible to see the decline as a matter not of historical inevitability but deliberate choice. Some policymakers were *attracted*, for a variety of reasons, to the idea that a service economy inevitably followed upon a manufacturing economy, as night follows day; that it was better simply to buy most of our goods from overseas. For America to turn away from manufacturing, for these thinkers, was simply another sign of America's front-of-the-pack position on a historical-developmental road race to who knows where. Others pursued what has been called "the financialization of the economy," in which the site of decision-making shifted, in effect, from the complex interactions between union and management and government, to Wall Street.

This shift was itself aided by two Midwestern institutions. One was the Chicago trading pits, where futures trading grew explosively in the wake of the 1973 publication of the Black-Scholes mathematical model. This model made it easier to quantify the amount of risk one took on in betting on changes in commodity prices. Politically, its effect was to change futures, options, and derivatives trading from a tool that allowed farmers to spread out their financial risk among other interested parties to a massive part of the economy that, by sheer size, exerted power over farmers' choices and incomes.

The other was the group of economists centered on the University of Chicago. They varied in approach and methodology, but seemed to coalesce around the idea that markets should be allowed to develop naturally rather than being planned. Since an industrial economy is *always* planned—again, mass production means standard gauges and road sizes and methods for getting the public to want things—this amounted, in practice, to an argument for letting the peddlers of financial products and services plan the economy instead. (Their whole job, after all, is allocating capital.) Since these people are even less likely to know how to manage a society than the CEO of Ford, the triumph of the Chicago argument has meant, in practice, two generations of bad planning, done on the fly by people who have no loyalty to any particular community, and who know that—when misfortune arrives—they get a bailout.

Why would anyone, even an economist, choose this system? I am reminded of the work of Andreas Malm, mentioned earlier. He showed, again, that coal-powered steam—for all its inevitability-in-retrospect—was simply not the best option for powering factories at the time when owners chose it. Water power could have done the job. What coal allowed was control. You chose the siting of factories. You closed up shop and went elsewhere if you saw some fractional advantage in doing so—or if your workers complained about their wages.

The financialization of the economy effected a similar transfer of power: workers could now be left out of the huddle. The economy of the U.S. became, once again, a matter of Eastern speculators viewing the vast fund to the west with bemusement and some contempt, trying to figure out what to do with it. The cities, certainly, were too large, too full of old plants; there was altogether too much countryside, which needed to be consolidated into a few large farms. The people who lived there, bereft of labor power or even labor, could seek retraining, or get addicted to Oxycontin, which it was now easier to market.

To the rich, and to authoritarian personalities of any class, this state of affairs is desirable *in itself*. Democracy strikes many people as inelegant; certainly, it is messy. And there are always those who require that the world provide them with people to lick their boots, or with boots to lick. For such people, the new financialized economic order that emerged from the 1980s *is* a utopia. It is where they want to live, either because it serves them or because they like it. And so once again, the Midwest—in this case the economics department at the University of Chicago—was the source of, and testing ground for, a possible future, this time one that profoundly destabilized the region's economy even as it reduced the hegemonic Midwestern power that writers like Hutton had once celebrated.

In the late 1990s, someone looked at a spreadsheet and decided that it made economic sense to close the refinery that employed 300 people in my hometown. That place stank so bad on summer days that you'd struggle to breathe. Neither it nor its parent company has a role to play in the future of the Midwest, if that future is to take place on a planet that warms less than two degrees over the next century. It has already left the town groundwater pollution that will take decades to fix. But this is the paradox of living or dying by what somebody with a spreadsheet thinks. A person might find themselves resenting the blitheness with which someone else takes away the problem that pays you a salary.

Farming faced its own disaster. Midwestern farmers from the late nineteenth century forward had argued, in regional newspapers and trade journals, for the right to feed the world.

Kristin Hoganson argues that "Midwest isolationism" is as much of a myth as Midwest egalitarianism. As far back as the late nineteenth century, regional farmers wrote about needing to outcompete white farmer-settlers in South America on the global market—after all, those immigrants had nicer temperatures and richer soil to work with.

But this global reach also made Midwestern farmers more vulnerable to the vicissitudes of national and global politics. Since more vulnerability is the *last* thing farmers need, New Deal farm policies had tried to limit this vulnerability. One of their practices was to pay farmers, when prices rose too high, to keep some land *un*used, and to buy, during good years, excess grain which could be saved for lean years. These policies evened things out somewhat for both farmers and consumers, and at least somewhat hedged against the kind of overfarming that had helped create the Dust Bowl. But some people think that "evening things out" is a bad policy goal.

Enter Earl Butz, the Secretary of Agriculture under Richard Nixon—and a former food company executive. (It was thoroughly consistent with Nixon's philosophy of government to hire a fox to regulate a henhouse.) Butz, a Midwestern boy (he had grown up on a dairy farm and worked at Purdue University), wanted farmers to produce on as large a scale as possible—his oft-quoted maxims included "Plant fence row to fence row" and "Get big or get out." (It was Butz who inspired the Kentucky farmer-poet Wendell Berry to write 1977's *The Unsettling of America*, his classic polemic in defense of small farms and local food. Every third person at your farmer's market has read Wendell Berry.) Big harvests meant low commodity prices for the sorts of food companies whose interests he represented. Large farmers reaped a bonanza for a few years in the early 1970s, after the U.S. weakened its currency and, in 1972, reached a lucrative deal to sell wheat to the Soviets—a deal that Butz advocated because he knew that it would reduce Midwestern farmers' opposition to this new direction in farm policy. The region's farmers, and others, took this money and used it to do what Butz said he wanted them to do—they bought new land and new equipment. (Get big or get out.)

But the massive inflation of the 1970s also seemed to demand a government response. Economists attribute this inflation to various causes; as with any argument about economic history, it's also an argument about politics, about who you think had the most power to make a thing happen or prevent an ill effect, and who you think it's ethical to hold responsible. The argument that seems most persuasive to me is the one that blames the era's inflation on Lyndon Johnson, who decided to go to war simultaneously against poverty, and against the people of Vietnam. All that government money, dumped on the country's various industries, some of it intended for munitions and other equipment and some of it intended to alleviate poverty, pushed commodity prices higher and higher, with nothing to bring them down, creating a spiral that was tough to break without raising taxes, something it is politically hard to do. The obvious solution to this dilemma, of course, would have been to continue to bombard poverty, which deserved it, while leaving alone the people of Vietnam, who did not.

Be that as it may. In 1980, then again in 1981, the Federal Reserve, directed by Paul Volcker, increased interest rates rather abruptly and threw the country into recession. He did reduce inflation, along with American aspirations and quality of life. (My father hunted work for months, until he got a job at a place called Pizza King, from which he returned home reeking pleasantly of pepperoni.) During the Volcker Recession, Midwestern farmers found themselves paying off, at higher rates, the loans they'd taken out for land that was now worth less. The money they used to pay it came from the sales of food, of course, and we had lost the Soviets as a customer, because, after the 1980 invasion of Afghanistan, the U.S. imposed sanctions upon them. Historian Osha Gray Davidson aptly describes these years as beginning the process of the "ghettoization" of rural communities. Town after town lost the concentration of small and midsized farms that anchored the place's economy.

The consolidation of farms was also a disaster for the non-human ecosystem. Row-crop agriculture—in which farmers use a large, likely gas-guzzling seed driller to plant massive amounts of soya or corn, in rows wide enough for the machines to pass through—uses up soil fairly quickly since the heavy tread of the machines packs it down, and the large portions left bare tend both to dry and bake in the sun and wash away in the rain. You then wind up with chemical fertilizer, borne by this dirt, leaching into water hundreds of miles away or getting into waterways and unstitching whatever ecological web exists there. Huge farms are also dirty—when you pack chickens together with "efficiency" in mind, what you get are animals that live in filth and are prone to getting sick. ("Debeaking" is a common practice—chickens won't normally peck each other to death with adequate space, but when they are packed together like styrofoam peanuts, they get nasty.)

Putting antibiotics in the animals' feed is one way to keep them growing on schedule. In its impossible, short, torturous, beakless, shit-covered life, we wouldn't want the poor chicken getting a *cold*. However, these farms' reliance on antibiotics have made them the site of an arms race between antibacterial drugs and bacteria, which bacteria will likely, sooner or later, win. The human health results of *that* eventuality might make some of us envy the chickens.

All of this happened, again, to make the members of Earl Butz's class richer.

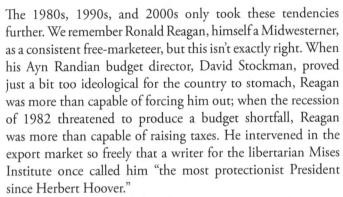

The 1980s, 1990s, and 2000s only took these tendencies further. We remember Ronald Reagan, himself a Midwesterner, as a consistent free-marketeer, but this isn't exactly right. When his Ayn Randian budget director, David Stockman, proved just a bit too ideological for the country to stomach, Reagan was more than capable of forcing him out; when the recession of 1982 threatened to produce a budget shortfall, Reagan was more than capable of raising taxes. He intervened in the export market so freely that a writer for the libertarian Mises Institute once called him "the most protectionist President since Herbert Hoover."

The former Illinois lifeguard *was* consistent about one thing, however: reducing the power of workers. His famous decision to fire air traffic controllers after a 1981 walkout remained absolutely central to his vision of his own presidency. Years later, when the resulting lack of trained personnel had become a threat to safety, a member of Reagan's own party, Representative Guy Molinari, tried to pass a bill that would simply allow one thousand of the better-trained ex-strikers to go back to work in the industry. To get their jobs back, they would have to prove that they hadn't been labor leaders.

Even this incredibly modest concession proved too much for Reagan. He responded with positively Nixonian pettiness, threatening not to allow tourists from Molinari's district to visit the White House anymore. When Molinari turned his law into an amendment to a 1986 spending bill, Reagan *invited a government shutdown* by vetoing that bill. Not only that, but he risked being late to his famous Iceland summit with Mikhail Gorbachev in order to sign the veto.

Reducing worker power was more important to Reagan than "freeing markets" as such. It was, apparently, at least as important to him as ending the Cold War. And it certainly mattered more to him than a trifling concern like the physical safety of travelers. And he described it all in homespun language that painted yet another utopian picture; he sold Chicago economics in brilliantly kitschy poetry.

Reagan's priorities should be questioned, but not his success in imposing them. The willingness of a Democratic president, in the following decade, to court the combined rage of the Midwest's unions and its farmers by advocating the North American Free Trade Agreement shows how much Reagan had succeeded in reshaping the outlook even of his opponents. It soon became received wisdom that "global competition" had undone the Midwest, though the Midwest has always been part of some global system of trade. This language implied that the Midwest lacked evolutionary fitness, a concept that ethical people don't apply to their fellow humans. This language also denied the element of choice at every level of the system.

In his 2015 study *Boom, Bust, Exodus*, sociologist Chad Broughton traces the story of Maytag, once a major employer for the city of Galesburg, Illinois. Seeking relevance, 1990s-style, the company hired its first-ever outside CEO, Lloyd Ward, because he had promised to increase the company's stock price. That measure was then taken as the ultimate and only relevant indicator of a company's viability. His obsession with stock price led to rumors that Ward was not only ignoring the quality control that had ensured Maytag's longevity, but conspiring with board members to sell off the company itself. Morale plummeted—though some of this darkened mood can also be blamed on the unwillingness of some longtime employees, and Galesburg residents, to accept a black man as CEO. (Nothing, even the seemingly innocent and wholesome practice of distrusting the boss, is completely simple.) Nevertheless, the decline of Maytag and its eventual withdrawal from Galesburg must be partially blamed on the treatment of the company as a mere fund—that word again—for shareholder enrichment, at the expense of every other value.

In 2008—amid an economic crisis made vastly worse by deregulation signed into law by Bill Clinton—another Illinoisian briefly seemed to promise, or threaten, a shift back in the direction of the postwar order. He bailed out the auto industry, and in doing so reaped just enough gratitude from Midwestern voters to eke out a 2012 re-election victory there over the hilariously aristocratic Mitt Romney (son of a former Michigan governor). He visited Galesburg many times, and at one point in Broughton's book, he brags of the partial recovery of Midwestern manufacturing: "I know there's an old site right here in Galesburg, over on Monmouth Boulevard—let's put some folks to work!"

And yet Obama did not, finally, represent the return of worker power. He had learned the wrong lessons from the prairie President on whom he consciously modeled himself, Abraham Lincoln. He talked often of Lincoln's famous "team of rivals," of Lincoln's penchant for filling his cabinet with intellectual enemies. Obama thought that this meant that the best presidents are those who seek the truth that supposedly lies in the middle. He held this belief sincerely, and his Presidency is the story of a man who magnanimously undermined himself at every turn—seeking a "grand bargain" on entitlement reform, one that certainly would have hurt his supporters and his party more than it would his rivals; adopting a cumbersome and complex Republican blueprint for health-care reform (one that has proven, because of that very complexity, easy to sabotage); attacking critics to his left more vigorously than those to his right. Perhaps it was this same magnanimity toward opponents that led him to, in effect, abandon the Employee Free Choice Act, which would have begun to undo the effects of Reagan and Taft-Hartley.

But Lincoln's greatness was not only his compromises; it was also his capacity to be dragged to extremes, over his own protestations, by the Abolitionists, and his intransigence once dragged there. Lincoln had to be forced into greatness by people like Frederick Douglass and, in a way, by people like Jefferson Davis, who would not compromise in holding their own moldy positions. And Lincoln died precisely the sort of death that comes to a man who has, at last, also stopped compromising.

It is no exaggeration to say that the inegalitarianism of the past forty years—the results of which were also distributed unequally to different populations, with the result that some of the relatively unfortunate blamed their problems on the more unfortunate—resulted in Trump. But if his ascendance looks like an even worse future emerging, it is also the moment in recent world history that most feels like a departure from the world that the Chicago neoliberals built—the world in which Reagan's supposed victory over the Soviet Union had somehow ended history itself.

("The good news," a friend said to me soon after the election, "is that we still live within history. The bad news is that we still live within history.")

It *is* an exaggeration to say, as many have, that Trump's occasional gestures in the direction of protectionism make him the tribune of the forgotten white Midwestern worker. The working class isn't all that white these days, and will continue not to be. And many white poor people, like poor people in general, do not vote. Though Trump managed to attract more than 50 percent of those white working-class voters who *did* turn out in November 2016, his share of them was not nearly as commanding as his share of, say, white people making over $100,000 a year. To borrow and adapt an illustration from the writer and *Chapo Trap House* co-host Matt Christman (no relation)—himself a Wisconsinite—Trump owed his victory less to the white guy behind the counter at the McDonald's than to the owner of the store, his boss, who lives in a slightly nicer part of town, and who spends his Sundays cursing recreationally at football players who kneel during the anthem.

Trump won the Midwestern states in 2016, in part, because he bothered to contest them at all, while his opponent did not. But we cannot forget the *way* he contested them: lurid tales of a "real" America menaced by ethnic minorities and elite enemies. (One of his last campaign ads, made up almost entirely of images of wealthy Jews, made clear what he meant by "elites." That an increased emphasis on open nativism and anti-blackness in mainstream discourse has also placed American Jews back on the chopping block is clear from the fact that two of the deadliest anti-Semitic mass hate crimes have taken place post-Trump and were carried out by Trump supporters.) As I finish this book, he has just told four of the most honorable people in Congress—two of them Midwestern women—to go back where they came from. He means this in a sense that cannot be corrected by pointing out, as many have, that they are citizens.

He owes some of his support to the ersatz form of populism, for which we need another name, that has dominated American political conversation in recent decades. (It is to the Populist Party of the 1890s what brutal Mr. C. is to brave Agent Cooper.) A too-strong belief in one's own normalcy becomes precisely a belief in one's superiority. Normalness becomes a fetish, a performance, or a product.

The Midwest, because of its perceived averageness, has long been forced to play a symbolic role in this process. Artists and writers who do not sufficiently condescend to their audiences get brought to heel by invocations of mythical Peorians. Here in the real world, Peoria has several mosques and a halal restaurant, a famous museum, the oldest community theatre in Illinois, a small college. Historically, it was one of the region's most important distilleries: how dare you assume these people are no fun?

In fact people everywhere are strange. If you look at a person and see a known quantity, you are not seeing that person. You are seeing a phantom generated by your desire to have everything simple enough to grip, to move around, to compel. This is presumably true even of Trump, though he has done nearly everything it is possible to do to make a person feel that he is interacting with a body unsouled.

Trump panders to, but he does not represent, the voters of the Midwest. But Trump *is* the candidate who best represents the right-wing response to the climate crisis. As Greg Grandin has pointed out, that old idea of the frontier, which continued to define American identity for over a century after the Census Bureau reported the frontier closed—think of Kennedy's "New Frontiers"—really, finally, has closed, and it has closed because of climate change. We simply cannot economically expand forever in the old way; nature is asserting limits. So Trump argues, in his (let us say) impressionist style, that the American future consists only in locking down our possession of what we already have. Where the humanist says, "Let's build the best society we can, out of whoever happens to show up," Trump says, in effect, "America for the People Already Here."

When a federal court upholds a law that literally makes it a crime to give a child a cup of water in the desert; when Immigrants and Customs Enforcement abducts a child at an airport in order to force the (undocumented) parents to turn themselves in; when Border Patrol shoots people at the Mexican border with tear gas: that's the reactionary response to a warming world. It is a much simpler and more satisfying response than regulating energy companies or taxing carbon. It only has two problems. It is evil, and it will result in, if nothing else, the end of this country. People who want to live in such a world are already too querulous to make a society, even with each other, even if they get everything they want. Picture them trying to manage a baking earth, an evaporating Lake Superior riddled with Asian carp, a countryside full of feral bacteria and reeking of CAFOs that produce less food every year. It won't work. A fully achieved Fortress America would just be the Donner Party a day or two before the cannibalism starts.

On Election Night 2016, I looked around at my household and I made a plan. I would gather my friends, get a homestead in the country, and learn to shoot. We would live self-sufficiently, modeling a new, better world as the old world crumbled around us. If the Nazis showed up, I'd be ready to defend my outpost.

Almost everything about this urge was silly—except for the fear it arose from. I was not wrong to feel that circumstances constituted an emergency, for the country and for my particular household. My wife and I are college teachers; we both work with prisoners; she is part Latina, with at least one undocumented immigrant in the family tree. We were renting rooms at the time to two former students, both of them black, one of them Muslim. When you look at our social ties and personal loyalties, it's a list of what Trump hates. I was not wrong to feel I ought to do something, even something strenuous.

But what a *something!* What stands out about my protective instinct to retreat to the wilds of Michigan is not only its tragic propensity for backfire, but its abstractness, its inutility. It was a vision for keeping "people" safe, but not for keeping *these* people safe. First of all—as Ashley reminded me, in a cheerful but tired voice—we knew people in Ann Arbor, and knew nobody in the country. And second, my wife went on, she was not interested in sharing a house simultaneously with a gun *and* with a male adult who had a history of anxiety and depression. She cited statistics on gun suicides. She didn't fear for her safety, but for mine.

Ashley kindly refrained from stating the most obvious reason why this idea wouldn't work: I am not homesteader material. I am not a farm kid, though I grew up in a small town. I am far removed, on both sides, from pioneers of any kind. My parents did not keep a gun in the house, or hunt, or fish. I have no military experience. My aim sucks. Nor do I like guns. Nor do I think killing people is justifiable, except defensively. Nor do I like the country, really.

This urge has no place in my head. It did not grow there organically. It's an invasive plant.

If you're trying to be as practical as possible, to solve an immediate problem, and an idea comes to you, vivid and overwhelming and a little blurry on the details, like a strong dream in which you nevertheless can't quite make out anyone's face; and if that idea is the *one* idea that absolutely *won't* work— you are probably in the presence of an ideology. Ideology at its most successful feels like a good dream: it resolves exactly those tensions that can't be worked out in real life as it's presently arranged. Say you can't choose between good jobs in different cities; you dream that you're somehow in both places at once, or that both jobs are somehow fused. Say you can't choose between two lovers; you'll dream an impossible (and patient) amalgam of both.

So what ideology was at work in me that night? To want to go off not on *my* own, but on *our* own—to build a community on a sort of middle frontier, on one side of you an old civilization hardening like grandpa's arteries and on the other a pure but punishing wildness—that's Midwestern. My version of the fantasy simply combined the utopianism of the Rappites with the postmodern cynicism of the doomsday prepper—that group of people so in need of a frontier that they have created a new one, in time, forming their imaginations and habits around an apocalyptic hellscape that doesn't yet and may never exist.

The Midwest plays a special role in the prepper's dream. A company named Vivos xPoint has acquired a network of old military bunkers in the Black Hills of South Dakota, which they have refurbished rather smartly, so as to offer, according to the website, "accommodations for more than 5,000 like-minded survivalists." (I wonder what, or who, these survivalists—a group notoriously riven by schism—are "like-minded" about.) If the dream of the company's owners comes true, the Black Hills really will be the center of all that is, in a way the Lakota never intended. In the photos, the curving steel walls are softened by wood-paneled cabinets and high-end couches—they have the cyborg look of the future utopia-dystopias you see in '70s sci-fi, that combination of unforgiving, mathematical silver and organic brown. The sticker price is a surprisingly low $35,000, plus another thousand a year. As with a vacation timeshare, it's the monthly fees that really get you.

The corporation has systems in place to ensure that each section of the compound will feature an equal mixture of necessary skills—all doctors and no plumbers, notes the website, with what I hope is gruesome irony, would be a "real disaster." The website also refers rather ominously to a "New Genesis," the new humanity that will emerge from these steel underground huts after the strategically undescribed Bad Thing has somewhat receded from the horizon. As with Turner, frontier-style adversity results in the evolution of, in effect, a new race.

The website adds, "We are not at liberty to discuss the ongoing security measures."

A missile silo in Kansas offers a slightly less messianic appeal. If Vivos xPoint subtly mixes biblical tropes into its sales pitch, Survival Condo is a strictly secular bit of territory. Its website masks the terrifying nature of the product on offer with an Eisenhoweresque prose style, mixing pseudo-military diction with boosterism—two dialects that evolved for the purpose of denying death. "Our objective when first approaching this project was to leave no stone unturned," runs one typical passage. Because Survival Condo is, in fact, a condo, it has an association and rules; during an emergency you'd have to work a four-hour day. Thomas More's Utopia required six, not only during emergencies.

ROW 6

STAYING WITH THE TROUBLE

The Midwest, it seems, even in supposed decline, still arrests the eye of the person who is concerned with testing out possible futures. A rich man with a half-assed vision of a "New Genesis" wants to return to the heart of all that is. And some people who concern themselves with climate change predict, too, that the region will soon find itself more popular than at any time since its postwar noon.

One news story tells you, if you are worried about climate change, to move to Pittsburgh or the Twin Cities. Another quotes a scientist named John Nielsen-Gammon, who says, "Not only will the Midwest avoid many of the bad effects of climate change, it will experience most of the good effects: less extreme cold and a longer growing season." Others suggest, specifically, Minneapolis, Ann Arbor, Madison, Chicago, Cincinnati, Buffalo, Duluth, Detroit, Cleveland, Nappanee (IN), and Sault St. Marie. Another journalist, listing the Rust Belt's advantages over the Sun Belt, notes ominously that "Detroit does not have to worry about rising sea levels." Other writers congratulate us on the impact climate change will have on our staple crop:

> An alarming increase in global temperatures from Earth's changing climate could bring an unexpected benefit for

US farmers who grow corn, the nation's biggest crop. While hotter weather generally threatens to sap crops of needed moisture, data from Midwest corn-growing states suggests the region will see warmer summers with more humidity.. . . If the trend of the past half century extends for another fifty years, farmers in the Midwest may see bigger yields.

It's as though America at some point decided to make the myth of the Midwest true. It really *is* now the Future of America and Therefore Humanity in a brutal and depressing sense.

Then again, this Midwestern future may be somewhat overhyped as well. When we consider the larger picture, any talk of climate change's "good effects," for this region or any other, brings to mind a well-known apothegm from one of our era's greatest poets: *drunk driving may kill a lot of people, but it also helps a lot of people get to work on time, so, it;s impossible to say if its bad or not* (*sic*). Take our "increased corn yields." Yields that Midwestern farmers will sell . . . where? To whom? Transported by what? In the middle of how many resource wars or droughts? The excess of it to be dumped on which foreign country that was never allowed to develop its own market? The money transferred on devices requiring which unobtainable rare-earth metals for their batteries?

The same sorts of questions throng me when I listen to the pronouncements of those who see Midwest economic revival in the provision of "smart" cars, to run on "smart" roads, patrolled by "smart" drones. Such things will also require rare-earth metals for their batteries, obtained by predictable supply lines. These both seem like strange things to expect of this century.

Boosterism of this kind is a form of denial.

I learned in college to admire the kind of novelistic empathy that insists that every person has their reasons. This is true about human persons. Something I did not learn in college is that, under capitalism, there are non-human persons; we call them corporations. Here in the Midwest, one such person is named Cargill. (It is the richest privately-held such person in the country.) Its executive director, a man named Greg Page, is very worried about climate change. He says, in one report by the Risky Business Project:

> A changing climate will present new risks and new opportunities as we face the complex task of producing enough food, feed and fuel for a world on its way to 9 billion people. Given the importance of the Midwestern United States to the world's agricultural production, it would be irresponsible to dismiss these projections lightly.

What nice things Mr. Page says! Within his generally amoral class, he appears a relatively good guy simply for acknowledging the weather outside his window. Yet, even as Page, from of the overflowing goodness of his heart, serves on the board of an organization that pushes American business to produce better risk analyses, his company Cargill sets itself emission-reduction targets that don't include up to 90 percent of the damage Cargill does—that ignore, for example, all the methane its cows belch into the atmosphere. It's classic greenwashing.

I suppose I don't mind if corporations decide to force themselves to be one percent less terrible for the sake of PR. Or for the sake of the two or three seconds a day these people are forced to be alone with their thoughts, the forty-five minutes a day when they are allowed actually to *be*, in effect, three-dimensional characters; for those troubled moments, after they've slept their optimized seven-and-three-quarter hours (never forgetting, of course, to set the app that monitors the quality of their sleep), and they're drinking some nutrient-rich concoction of coffee and algae and butter and bonemeal, or whatever it is this month, and distractedly kissing their child on the head, and thinking *is this who I want to be?*; before they shove that consciousness aside, and put on a different, simpler self, the set of premises and preferences that they learned in business school: the consciousness of the corporate entity they serve, the hostile mind that they willingly invite into theirs. They think its thoughts after it.

These people, as I've said, are complex; they're not demons. But that consciousness—that assumed person they take on—is simple, and malevolent, and it will not fix this for us. It will cook the moral books as it cooks the planet. The persons we call corporations have no role in figuring out a role for the Midwest in a warmed planet; they can only mismanage things further, and they'll try. We cannot avoid dealing with them, but we can't leave things to them, or trust the operations of rational self-interest to discover the solution.

If the Midwest has unique advantages to offer this historical moment, it also faces extreme disadvantages. Our Midwestern cities, in many cases, have based their economies on chemicals, agribusiness, or energy. These corporations will need radical transformation, or destruction, and either way, they're going to work very hard distracting us from that fact.

Our existing infrastructure, yet another report tells us, is deeply unready for climate change. We could, of course, *fix* that, but infrastructure just makes you weak and dependent. If we build a sturdy tunnel, and a fast train to travel through that tunnel, then you might use that train to get to work every day, like some kind of weakling.

Other eyes turn to our Great Lakes—one of the world's largest freshwater sources. Their presence assures us that external capital will flow toward the region. (Nestlé, at the moment, is bottling that water, at almost no cost to anyone but the residents of Michigan.) To exactly the extent that capital finds a reward for its interest in the Lakes, of course, an incomparable natural resource is destroyed. Already the Lakes are menaced by algae blooms and dead zones, and by industrial wastes, ballast water from container ships (which carries invasive species), and the fertilizer from that row-crop agriculture mentioned earlier. Asian carp are prevented from entering and devastating the Lakes yet again by a single, malfunctioning barrier.

Water and jobs are depleting so quickly in the Ogallala Aquifer region, under Nebraska, that scholar Deborah Popper has seriously, and rather credibly, proposed that we think of the place going forward as a commons for buffalo. By this she doesn't mean that she intends for the place to be literally uninhabited, still less that we move people off of it forcibly (Native Americans who live in that area have been shoved around enough); she intends it as a kind of metaphor to guide thought. The idea is that a battered species and a damaged place can soothe each other back to health if humans will consent to live alongside them both lightly, carefully.

Some of our cities may soon be as hot as those of the South, and in some of our states, it's still legal for the power companies to cut you off for nonpayment during a lethal heat wave. (This would be a good thing to bug your city council about.) Our climate is so unstable year to year that our fruit plants don't know when to bud—they pop out, only to freeze to death. The weather, like the country, is polarizing: more frequent and intense droughts, but also more of the kinds of storms that wreck a city.

And there's the almost impossible problem of deciding what to do about places that no longer constitute a large fund to anyone in particular, but that still have people in them, that are still loved: the towns and small cities. We have to find ways to make our East Liverpool, Ohios, and our Alma, Michigans, vital places to live, and we have to find ways to do it that don't involve burning more carbon or destroying the last of our topsoil. I not only don't have a one-size-fits-all solution to that problem; I'd worry about anyone who thought they did. Solutions, if any, will emerge from the ground up, from the work of responsible and thoughtful and kind people working together.

In the course of my research for this book, I discovered that my hometown has been the subject of at least two Ph.D. dissertations, both of them in the first half of the twentieth century. One of the scholars involved selected Alma because it so perfectly represented the kind of Midwestern "country town" that was both historically new and important to a distinctive pattern of American economic development. The pattern is *so* generally American that the other dissertator calls the town Blankton: it is a cipher, a stand-in for America-in-general. No wonder I have trouble describing it to my wife.

Reading up on the town's more recent fortunes, I found only news stories about pollution and the loss of jobs and stores, and, intriguingly, an essay that appeared in a small literary journal. The author celebrates precisely the town's representative powerlessness, describing it as "a small town in the middle of Michigan that's struggling to hang on." He exclaims over the "fathomless depths" of the window of the men's clothing store (closed since 2009), listens to the "ragged arpeggios" of the wind-driven fast-food bags that collect behind the Wal-Mart where my dad used to work, contemplates the "demonic and naive" face of the statue in front of the Big Boy's where I ate after my high school all-night party. In this restaurant he feels "in contact with something so overwhelmingly sad and American as to be indistinguishable from facing your own mortality." He proclaims several times his love for the town, which "burns eternity into your soul." He says that he could stay forever or "leave tomorrow," sounding far too much like a traveling salesman who is about to get someone pregnant and then skip town. Jogging, he accidentally startles two guys in camo who are in the middle of what I must imagine—remembering the deep homophobia of that place—was the most furtive of blowjobs.

Even in his attempts at sympathy, this writer treats the lost Midwestern small town as a place into which he wanders, from which he extracts an epiphany, and leaves. It is still a fund for somebody, even if it's just a fund of attractively literary abjectness. But then every writer risks doing that, including me. The chemical company that dumped the carcinogenic flame retardant into the ground, and probably my fatty tissues, and certainly my mom's, has certainly long since extracted what *it* needs, and left; forty-three years after the spill, it is still fighting one of the lawsuits. The person who owns a Midwestern patch of land and the person who intends to live there still represent, often enough, diametrically oppposed interests.

I could keep listing Midwestern environmental and cultural problems until I am as fearful as any prepper; until I, too, feel ideology overtaking me like a strong dream, imagine myself surrounded by destructive hordes. Maybe my imaginary hordes are angry white Trumpists, or oblivious white yuppies, rather than brown immigrants, but it's still not a fruitful way to approach the world. I am them. They are me. Mr. C is also the Agent Cooper who seeks to thwart him.

And this apocalyptic time into which we have been born is also a time that gives us a power never enjoyed by anyone in history. Unlike someone living in 1910, with two horrendous wars still ahead, we know, with great precision, what is coming; and we know that though we can't stop all of it, that *every bit we do stop, or delay, or mitigate, represents millions of people saved.* No other generation has been afforded such a scope for *consciously* doing good.

Perhaps we fear that power, that responsibility, as much as we fear apocalypse. Certainly, when we obsess about the latter—as I have risked doing here—we shirk the former. Despair and nihilism about our situation are also ways of giving up, of refusing to pull one's weight; they are even less helpful than naive boosterism or denial.

So I look for helpful ways to frame our future, and immediately, I find several Midwestern resonances in an article that I have long found one of the most provocative attempts to think through the next few centuries.

Peter Frase's "Four Futures" (2011) shocked me when I first read it because of the confidence with which it asserts: "One thing we can be certain of is that capitalism *will* end." A person who thinks a lot about the ecological realities I've been describing in the past few sections may be tempted to agree too quickly: Sure. Capitalism will end *us*. But Frase means something different. He takes the end of capitalism not as a terminal point but as a place to start out from. Like Thomas Hutchins surveying out from that little stick in the wilderness, he thinks he's at the beginning of a world, not the end of one. What does he find out there?

As the essay's title suggests, he sees four possibilities, which result from the combination of four factors: egalitarianism, hierarchy, abundance, and scarcity. So, for example, you could have what he calls socialism: egalitarianism plus scarcity. His socialism is a kind of future worldwide Cuba in which ecological disaster, not the United States, imposes sanctions and forces rationing. It's still a lot better than what he calls rentism: hierarchy plus abundance. Imagine a society that runs on "complete automation and free energy," but with you paying a license fee for every molecule of sustenance or moment of pleasure, till you're too far indebted ever to retire. When a giant ag company patents every corn gene they manage to map, so that every seed-saving farmer is a bootlegger: rentism is that, but for everything.

We might imagine, for example, a future Columbus, Ohio, in which people live in abandoned trailers stacked together in a sort of grid formation, playing video games all the time. This is the setting of the 2018 movie *Ready Player One*, based on the 2011 novel by Ernest Cline. The movie relocates the action of the story from Oklahoma City to the Midwest, as though to make its vision of America in the year 2045 more representative, more generally *middle*. It's about a somewhat generic nerd who plays video games constantly. (I note that, in Frase's projected rentist future, many elements of labor have been "gamified"—you might mine an element or fight a war virtually, via drone, in a kind of pretend game. The film does not imply this, but it's consistent with the film's presentation.) Everyone in this future Columbus lives in a state of joyless compulsion and wired exhaustion, like people who can't put their phones down long enough to sleep.

On the other hand, socialism and rentism both beat Future #3: hierarchy plus scarcity. "[W]hat if resources and energy are simply too scarce to allow everyone to enjoy the material standard of living of today's rich?" Frase asks. If we arrive in such a situation with social conditions as polarized between rich and poor as they are now, what we'll end up with is murder-by-terrible-working-conditions, at best—the conditions enforced by official brutality—or murder-as-such, at worst. He calls it exterminism, and we can see a foreshadowing of it in some American and European approaches to immigration: cook the climate, throw the refugees in prison.

Frase's own example of what an exterminist future would look like is another science fiction movie set partly in the Midwest, 2011's *In Time*. In that film, it's the year 2169, and, due to genetic engineering, you must accrue credit in order to *not* die the moment you turn twenty-six. It is a gruesome extension of the idea of living paycheck-to-paycheck. In Dayton, most people are within a day of running out and must slave to stay alive.

Frase's fourth future—abundance plus egalitarianism—he calls, with a winningly puckish indifference to the word's real-world history, communism. It shares a name, though not necessarily much else, with the thing Ronald Reagan supposedly buried, the thing that, in its failing, ended history. Frase's model for such a high-tech communism is also, in its way, Midwestern—it's the Starfleet of *Star Trek*, that drama about a cocky Iowan, Jim Kirk. I want to believe in Frase's fourth future, but people with other skills than mine will have to figure out how to provide the abundance. The possibility of decoupling—of figuring out a way to deliver consistent economic growth while reducing not just the rate at which our carbon consumption increases (that might be doable), but our actual total usage of the stuff—seems far-off if not impossible at the moment. All I know is we'll need the egalitarianism.

In her later writing on the subject, Deborah Popper has emphasized the metaphorical quality of the Buffalo Commons—that it's supposed to help us frame an overall attitude. Her idea poses a question for me: How should we think of the Midwest in general, in this parlous time, when it seems likely to serve as an ark of survival to many?

I will not call it a heartland—for I am not a general planning a war. I will not call it Middle America, for that is meaningless.

I *almost* want to propose that we think of it as a moral frontier: that we transfer the energy, the excitement, that has traditionally surrounded the idea of the frontier (at least for white people) to the project of living generously, peaceably, and inclusively with our neighbors, old and new, human, animal, and plant. That we apply the idea of going *beyond* the limits of our current moral and political maps to the project of living decently *within* our physical limits—without throwing anyone else away. People will want to live here; those of us who already do have been given a chance to respond to this influx with a decency and humaneness that would, if we attained it, mark a new spot on the map of what humans can do.

The idea of the American frontier is so violent and colonial that I can propose this metaphor only ironically: as though I were a pacifist proposing war upon war. But of course that is a venerable maneuver among pacifists. William James called his idea for a national service corps "the moral equivalent of war" because he knew that only war, up to that point in human history, had brought people together in the numbers and with the level of organization needed to build lasting peace, and that humanity's only hope was to bring that same energy to the prevention of war by the generous provision of services. Old metaphors, in a new context, can also have a transformative power; dead and deadening concepts can become part of a life-giving possibility.

The Midwest, to remain a livable place, in a hotter world, using (most likely) less energy—if economic growth can be decoupled in an absolute sense from carbon pollution, I'll be as happy as anyone, but it seems a stupid bet to take—with the large number of people who will be brought to live here by climate change, will need to find a way of thinking about this task that arouses the same can-do spirit that the frontier once did. We may be done with physical frontiers, but we need people who live out beyond the typical, who inhabit a moral frontier, if, for sentimental reasons, we want some version of civilization to exist in this region in the hot year 2120.

Our history, which we carry with us unknowingly, as soil does, includes many failures; it is mostly failure. It also includes many examples of people who crossed moral, and sometimes physical, frontiers for the sake of conscience, people whose goodness transcended their era's norm, sat beyond it on the map.

It includes the abolitionists who rushed to make Kansas a free state.

It includes the Native Americans who rushed to defend Standing Rock against yet another pointless and destructive oil pipeline—all of them, historically speaking, victims of the idea of the frontier.

It includes the churches that are hiding undocumented people.

It includes the Michigan antifa who chased the white supremacist Richard Spencer out of Lansing, resulting in the cancellation of his planned university speaking tour. ("Where were you?" the reader asks. We had to move that day, and my wife wouldn't let me have the car. I don't blame her, but I still feel sheepish about it.)

It includes the people who stealthily plant trees and copses and who take care of the soil, knowing that these have the potential to capture far more carbon than any human-made technology currently on the market.

It includes the people who camp out at every city council meeting, for years, until the mayor finally agrees to impose effective civilian oversight on the city police, and puts actual poor people on the oversight board.

It includes the people who spend dozens of hours a week that they don't have to spend, shutting down a fracking permit.

It includes the people who, during a heat snap, let strangers sleep on their couch, because in the unaccommodated heat, or without air conditioning, they will die.

It includes the people who stop to film incidents of police violence or ICE harassment with their phones.

It includes the people who organize their workplaces.

And it includes the people who allow themselves to be politically polarized—again, polarization is inescapable when interests vary this much—without letting it turn them *morally* Manichean. Even as we fight a battle that has only two sides, we each remain, at our best and worst, far more than two-sided. This does not mean that I think anyone should try to compromise with Trump or soften their opposition. I want to beat the side that Trumpists align themselves with. But one reason I do so is that Trumpists are as doomed in that America, that Midwest, as everyone else.

In my religious tradition, we are told to love our enemies. We are *not* told to pretend we have none. The reason is obvious: once you've named your enemies as such, the duty of loving them stands out clearly, named and unavoidable. The political polarization that marks our moment is not going away, and it *shouldn't* go away; there really are important conflicts to settle, about which people from the same family, people who love each other, differ fundamentally. (Polarization, not conciliation, ended slavery.) In lieu of bemoaning it, as middle-of-the-road liberals do, I would propose that we speak honestly about who our enemies are, under which circumstances, and what kinds of duties this acknowledgement imposes on us. It's a serious responsibility, having an enemy. Not for babies.

On the moral frontier, you wrestle with things that are too big for you, and sometimes you fail.

In the weeks and months that followed November 2016, I tried to figure out healthy and useful ways to respond to the Trumpian interruption of the end of history. I joined the Democratic Socialists of America; I adapted my syllabus to include more readings about climate change; I threw myself into my union at work; I found local religious groups that offered sanctuary to the undocumented, and spent some volunteer hours with them. I started to learn about the plants native to my area and thinking about where I could place some. (Lawns exist mainly to waste water, and crabgrass doesn't store carbon in the soil as well as most native plants will.) I started showing up to my city council meetings, doing research to learn the extent of our collaboration with Immigrants and Customs Enforcement (the people who snatch undocumented grandmothers from hospitals). I started learning about things like "Whether my state government allows energy companies to shut off people's power during extreme weather events," since such events will grow more common in the coming years. (Emily Johnston's essay "We Have to Stop Pretending That Solving Climate Change is Complicated" points to a number of moves that cities, towns, and states can make that will decrease pressure on ecosystems; energypolicy.solutions/ guide provides a similar agenda for the federal government.)

As I have done all of these things, I have realized, slowly, that I have to go on doing them, and similar things, knowing that they are not enough.

My mom had an operation a few months ago. She lost a third of her left lung. She is fine, and also not fine. The part of her that contained a slow-growing tumor is gone, and her biopsy report had nothing but good news. She is seventy-five years old.

I enjoyed seeing my family, as, despite conflict, I always do. Remember the awful, interminable "empathy" debates that surrounded the 2016 election? An editorialist would write something to the effect that "We [who?] need to empathize with Trump supporters." Someone else would respond, reasonably, "I don't need to empathize with people who want to put me in an ICE camp." A third person would respond less helpfully—"I can't wait for those hicks to die"—and so on, ad infinitum. The most useful intervention in this conversation was probably the work of the Kansas writer Sarah Smarsh, who pointed out that "Trump voters" had gotten conflated with the entire white portion of the working class, whom you should very much feel bad for, insofar as they are working-class.

My family is working-class. They also voted for Trump. And as much as I love them, this makes me angry—it feels like a conflict of a different order than I've had with them before. The degree of anger differs from person to person. My sister, it turns out, still has limits: the policy of family separation made her angry enough to call her congressional rep. My mom, I think, finds the world overwhelming and confusing and votes for the guy who will get rid of abortion; that issue is her moral lodestone.

To keep my anger in perspective, I think about the fact that if Hillary Clinton had won, I would be complicit in whatever idiotic wars she started, and whatever further banking deregulation she insisted upon, and whatever "smart" enhancements of the police state she introduced; I voted for her, already planning to protest a lot of things she did.

Still, the anger is there. I drove into town rehearsing futile counterarguments, knowing they were futile. When my father told what I considered to be a fatuous anecdote about William F. Buckley, that indefatigable friend to Latin America's rapists and torturers, a man who would definitely call the cops if my father happened to take a walk through his neighborhood, I snapped at him. I tried to remember why I was there: my mom was about to have a traumatic operation, and we needed to work smoothly together to get her through it. But other people are also having traumatic operations, and ICE is barging into those operations to put other people's moms in detention. I didn't feel like I should forget that, either.

I am not smart enough or good enough to hold these two things in my head.

On the day of the operation, it was just my dad, my sister, my mom, and me, in a hospital in Grand Rapids. I realized that I couldn't remember the last time the four of us had been together without any in-laws, any grandchildren. My sister was efficient. My dad was terrified and sympathetic. My mom was drugged and looked like a chew toy that had been lost at sea.

This is the part where it's tempting to write "in that moment, politics fell away, and pragmatics/common sense/simple values took over," but that sort of sentence is a lie. Your politics and your pragmatics, your common sense, your simple values, are a series of Russian nesting dolls that contain each other. My politics in that moment was that my mom had spent her life doing the best she could with the information she had, and that her best had done harm and so had mine.

Now my mother is at home, dealing with her still-aching lungs, with only my dad to help. I left after a week because I had to work, had to see my wife again. Mom never thought to ask me to stay more days, but she could have used me. I am inadequate. I took on more than I could do, and I failed. That is what people do on the edge of something. Perhaps this is one of the gifts that family gives us: a lifelong confrontation with the fact that we will only, at best, lovingly fail the people who were counting on us most.

This historical moment invites us to begin a long transformation of the Midwest: from fund to place; from a speculator's toy to a crowded but ultimately accommodating home for whoever needs it. It invites us to construct a *we* that everyone can wear. It invites us to think about utopia again, and to lovingly fail at building it.

And we must do this in a Midwest where the time seems less noon than midnight. Anyone who has lived through a

Midwestern small-town childhood knows something about midnight, though: there are whole years when it's the most interesting time of day. It's the time when all kinds of new possibilities seem like they might be hovering somewhere nearby, precisely because in the dark you remember how little of this flat place you ever truly see. It's the feeling Theodore Roethke describes in "Night Journey":

> *Now as the train bears west,*
> *Its rhythm rocks the earth,*
> *And from my Pullman berth*
> *I stare into the night*
> *While others take their rest.*

When I was a teenager—wanting that feeling, that staring while others rest—I stayed up late whether or not I had a reason, and when I could get away with it, I walked around. I was always depressed as a teenager. After all, if the place I lived in was normality incarnate, then human normality itself was the wrong fit for me. This was an irrational amount of weight to place on the results of such a small sample size, but I didn't know that then. I couldn't know that then; a dot doesn't know width. And anyway it was deeper than that: If history seemed like something that happened to other people, located elsewhere, so did the future. I had no expectations for it; it hadn't even occurred to me to have expectations for it. It was like the cross-country course at my school, a punishing flat expanse that you'd look at and see your physical torture continued forever.

Sometimes, with friends—when I had friends—I'd sit on top of the low-slung roof of the Catholic church in my town, a strange building, equal parts Hobbiton, Sagrada Familia, and Pizza Hut. I learned decades later that it had been designed by the American son-in-law of Joseph Stalin. He had married

Stalin's daughter, Svetlana Alliluyeva, after her defection, then run off with her money, *then* joined an architecture-based cult led by Frank Lloyd Wright's widow. At some point in this trajectory he paused over our farm town and built this place, a building in which, as I then understood matters, people played bingo and tried to work their way into heaven by praying to Mary. (*My* family attended a fundamentalist Baptist church at the edge of town, where we celebrated, among other things, our deliverance from Catholics' errors. Our roof sucked, though.) My friends and I knew none of this history as we sat there, discussing I can no longer imagine what; such was my sense of that town's impermeability to history that I would have had no way to assimilate that fact even if someone had told it to me.

Sometimes I walked over to the 76 gas station, where two friends of mine—slightly older; readers of *Film Threat* and Lester Bangs; smokers of weed; and havers, even, so they said, of sex—worked the night shift and held a kind of impromptu salon for teenage dirtbag *philosophes* such as myself. One evening as we sat talking, a guy I vaguely knew stopped to buy milk. This person had graduated high school early, a fact I found fascinating. Why would you accelerate a timeline to nowhere in that way? Why rush your way through an asymptote? So I asked him about it, how it worked, what he was up to now. We got to talking. We walked to his house, and he, rather artlessly, spoke a truth about his life that was simultaneously so obvious and so personal that I'd never acknowledged that it was also the truth of mine: *I had to get out of here. It's so lonely.*

Any labor organizer could predict what happened next. He had named a shared problem; I added to his description. Gradually, a plan took shape. Would I have eventually figured my way to college without that conversation? Probably—for lack of better ideas. My only alternative was to work with my father at Wal-Mart. That version of me, in that alternate universe, has failed to adjust to that life with my father's stoicism—the stoicism that his father beat into him, and that my father refused, using all his might, to beat into me. That version of me spent his thirties so sore he could barely move. Possibly the opiates (initially prescribed) have killed him by now.

Every human is so many other humans—and you feel that in the Midwest, wandering through those squares, among those people who, on paper, could have been you. Opening the door of your house you feel as though it is yours by some inconceivable coincidence: this and not the others. You feel doubled, cloned. You feel déjà vu in your own subjectivity. This feeling, like our history, points more than one way. It can make you ingrown like a toenail—*why can't I get the break I'm supposed to?* But it can also cause you to think of those other selves: that poorer self, that queerer self, that darker self, that privileged self, that self who is kind of racist and watches too much TV but who has lost his mobility working at the refinery and whose body is full of flame retardant, that self who is a wheelchair-bound black lesbian, also full of flame retardant. It can tell you that you must try to care for all those selves as though they were you—as though you were made from the same soil and headed back to it. In this deep, clotted, night-black, dirt-black dark, who even knows for sure who *they* are, who *I* am? Or who *we* might yet be?

ACKNOWLEDGMENTS

I thank the Christmans, Clarks, Naps, Lucases, and Eckmans for being my family and supporting my writing, even when this means getting argued with in public, or losing control over anecdotes involving oneself. I thank my dad, Phil Christman Sr., in particular, for the tidbit about Stalin's daughter, which inspired me to pitch a review of recent books about the Midwest. I thank B.D. McClay for instead commissioning a full essay, from which this book evolved. I thank her and the *Hedgehog Review* for editing, polishing, publishing, and promoting that essay. I thank the guilds of people who study the Midwest professionally— the Midwestern History Association and the Society for the Study of Midwestern Literature—for the respectful attention and engagement that they've given to someone who is neither a historian nor a full-fledged literary scholar; more importantly, I thank them for their work, without which mine couldn't exist. They are, as a group, interesting and unpretentious people who work hard and welcome outsiders—it's as though they were trying to live up to the best stereotypes about the place they study. The same is true of the writers who run Belt, my publisher, and of my fellow Belt authors, whom I have drawn upon freely. I thank the Institute for the Humanities at the University of Michigan for the fellowship during which I finished this book, and my colleagues for the incredibly useful feedback they provided in its late stages. I thank my union, LEO, for enabling me to make a full-time living teaching only three classes per semester, so that I don't have to take on a second job, which means that I could take a few hours a day pre- or post-work, and more hours during the summer, to write. I thank Adam and Erin, Christian and Beth, Brian and Amanda, Ian and Kelly, Tressie and Vivian, and many, many kind readers who have reached out to me via email or social media and, in a number of cases, become valued friends. You all give me someone to do this *for*. I thank Ashley for being a better wife, friend, and fellow-thinker than I imagined I would ever meet.

NOTES

One historian: Andro Linklater, *Measuring America* (New York: Plume, 2003), 2.

unassuming little obelisk: https://www.google.com/maps?ll=40.642392,-80.519378&q=40.642392,-80.519378&hl=en&t=m&z=15.

August 20, 1785: C. Albert White, *A History of the Rectangular Survey System* (Washington, D.C.: U.S. Government Printing Office, 1984), 17-19. https://www.blm.gov/sites/blm.gov/files/histrect.pdf. But note that surveyor Andrew Ellicott's journals and letters suggest the 23rd-24th. https://archive.org/details/andrewellicotthi00mathuoft/page/46. His account seems to be written closer to the actual date than Porter's journals, which give us the 20th but are written (I believe) after the fact; however, the wording of Ellicott's letters doesn't make clear whether he's crossing *to* or crossing *back*. The sources don't make it clear which survey team member actually left the stake.

The next day: William A. Porter, "A Sketch of the Life of General Andrew Porter," *The Pennsylvania Magazine of History and Biography* IV: 3 (1880), 277. https://archive.org/details/jstor-20084462/page/n1.

September 30: William D. Pattison, *Beginnings of the American Rectangular Land Survey System, 1784-1800* (Chicago, IL: University of Chicago Press, 1957), 119. https://archive.org/details/beginningsofamer00patt/page/119.

English style: Linklater 12.

This was a revolutionary concept: Linklater 4.

he envisioned each square: Hildegarde Johnson, *Order Upon the Land* (New York: Oxford University Press), 39.

The land is remarkably rich: Pattinson 130-31.

Soon after they began: Richard Butler, "Journal of General Butler" (Neville B. Craig, ed., *The Olden Times, Volume II*, Pittsburgh:

Wright and Charlton, 1848), 435. https://books.google.com/books?id=bC5KAQAAMAAJ&printsec=frontcover&source=gbs_ge_summary_r&cad=0#v=onepage&q&f=false.

clashing methodologies: Linklater 79.

property of FirstEnergy: "The 'Point of Beginnings'," *Farm & Dairy,* June 6, 2002, https://www.farmanddairy.com/news/the-point-of-beginnings-it-all-started-along-the-ohio-pa-border/6221.html.

Another source: Linklater 1, 6.

underwater: T.R. Witcher, "Setting the Boundaries: The Point of Beginning Survey," *Civil Engineering* 88 (7): 41.

hard to see especially: Michael Martone, *The Flatness and Other Landscapes* (Athens, GA: University of Georgia Press, 2000), 3.

a recent survey: Walt Hickey, "Which States Are in the Midwest," FiveThirtyEight, April 29, 2014 (https://fivethirtyeight.com/features/what-states-are-in-the-midwest/).

Mark Fisher: "What is Hauntology?" *Film Quarterly* 66:1 (2012), 16-24.

This Midwest: William H. Gass, *In the Heart of the Heart of the Country and Other Stories* (New York: Harper and Row, 1968), 186.

simply sickened: William H. Gass, *The Tunnel* (New York: Knopf, 1995), 135.

an abstract nowhere: Glenway Wescott, *Good-Bye, Wisconsin* (New York, NY: Harper, 1928), 39.

Tiya Miles: *The Dawn of Detroit* (New York: The New Press, 2017), *passim.*

less distinctive: Matthew Wolfson, "The Midwest Is Not Flyover Country," *The New Republic*, March 22, 2014, https://newrepublic.com/article/117113/midwest-not-flyover-country-its-not-heartland-either.

blurry landscape: Richard Longworth, *Caught in the Middle* (New York: Bloomsbury, 2008), 16.

geographic coherence: Andrew R. L. Cayton and Susan Gray, *The American Midwest* (Bloomington, IN: Indiana University Press, 2001), 1.

fuzzy, probabilistic: Daniel Montello, Michael Goodchild and Jonathan Gottsegen, "Where's Downtown?" *Spatial Cognition and Computation* 3 (2003): 185-204.

great body: Abraham Lincoln, "Second Annual Message to Congress," in *Lincoln: Political Writings and Speeches*, ed. Terence Ball (New York, NY: Cambridge University Press, 2013), 157.

heartland: Kristin Hoganson, *The Heartland: An American History* (New York: Penguin, 2019), xv.

Martone: *The Flatness* 33.

Marguerite Young: *Miss MacIntosh, My Darling* Vol 1 (Normal, IL: Dalkey Archive, 1993, orig. 1965), 4.

Meridel Le Sueuer: *North Star Country* (New York City: Duell, Sloan and Pearce, 1945), 38.

Nathan Beacom: "Is the Midwest Beautiful?" *The New Chicagoan*, Nov. 19, 2018, https://thenewchicagoan.com/blog/2018/11/18/is-the-midwest-beautiful.

Katy Rossing: "Smothered: American Nostalgia and the Small Wisconsin Town," *Hypocrite Reader*, January 2012, http://hypocritereader.com/12/smothered-american-nostalgia.

this bulk-purchasing: David R. Meyer, "Midwestern Industralization and the American Manufacturing Belt in the Nineteenth Century," *Journal of Economic History* 49:4 (1989), 921-937.

Willa Cather: *My Ántonia* (Boston, MA: Houghton Mifflin, 1954), 5. First published 1918. (Both quotes.)

flyover country: This supposed pejorative appears to have been popularized, if not invented, *by Midwesterners* reacting defensively to the region's supposed unpopularity in the coastal mind. See Gabe Bullard, "The Surprising Origin of the Phrase 'Flyover Country,'" *National Geographic*, March 14, 2016, http://news.nationalgeographic.com/2016/03/160314-flyover-country-origin-language-midwest.

Alec McGillis: "The Rust-Belt Theory of Low-Cost Culture," *Slate*, January 1, 2015, http://www.slate.com/articles/arts/culturebox/2015/01/cheap_high_culture_in_baltimore_buffalo_detroit_and_other_midsize_cities.html.

Fred Hampton: A good starting source is Jeff Gottlieb and Jeff Cohen, "Was Fred Hampton Executed?" *The Nation*, December 25, 1976, https://www.thenation.com/article/was-fred-hampton-executed/. They also killed Mark Clark. They nearly killed Hampton's girlfriend and unborn baby. And then they lied about it. These are facts to bear in mind the next time CPD claims that an unarmed black person "provoked" officers into shooting.

Andrea Lawlor: *Paul Takes the Form of a Mortal Girl* (New York: Vintage, 2018), 308.

worlds of their own making: Andrew R.L. Cayton, "The Anti-Region," in *The American Midwest*, 148.

Prince: Kenzie Bryant, "Prince Had No Time for Matt Damon's Small Talk," *Vanity Fair*, July 18, 2016, http://www.vanityfair.com/style/2016/07/matt-damon-prince-small-talk.

James Shortridge: *The Middle West* (Lawrence, KS: University Press of Kansas, 1989), 4-5.

counterfeiting: John Ervin Kirkpatrick, *Timothy Flint* (Cleveland, OH: Arthur H. Clark, 1911), 39.

link between North and South: Kenneth R. Winkle, "The Great Body of the Republic," in *The Identity of the American Midwest*, Andrew R.L. Cayton and Susan Gray, eds. (Bloomington, IN: Indiana University Press, 2007), 114.

happy mediocrity: Benjamin Franklin, "Information to Those Who Would Remove to America," https://founders.archives.gov/documents/Franklin/01-41-02-0391.

Frederick Jackson Turner: *The Frontier in American History* (New York: Henry Holt, 1920), 16.

task of the Middle West: Turner 155.

Cahokia: Timothy Pauketat, *Cahokia* (New York: Penguin, 2009), 4.

David Treuer: *Rez Life* (New York: Grove/Atlantic, 2012), 6-7.

the heart of everything that is: Julie A. Rice-Rollins, "The Cartographic Heritage of the Lakota Sioux," *Cartographic Perspectives* 48:4 (2004), 45.

Great Lakes country: John L. Riley, *The Once and Future Great Lakes Country* (Toronto: McGill-Queens UP, 2014), 14-18.

Richard White: *The Middle Ground* (New York: Cambridge UP, 1990), 1.

their numbers actually grew: David Treuer, *The Heartbeat of Wounded Knee* (New York: Penguin/Random House, 2019), 48.

Willam Hogeland: *Autumn of the Black Snake* (New York: Farrar, Straus, and Giroux, 2017), 376.

vaccines were available: Treuer, *Wounded Knee*, 91.

Reagan . . . communism: Edmund Morris, *Dutch* (New York: Random House, 1999), 158.

no one can count all our military bases: Nick Turse, "America's Empire of Bases 2.0," *The Nation* Jan. 10, 2011, https://www.thenation.com/article/americas-empire-of-bases-20/.

Roy M. Robbins: See Chapter 1 of Robbins's survey of the American public domain, *Our Landed Heritage* (1942), here: http://www.ditext.com/robbins/land1.html.

Ray Allen Billington: "The Historians of the Northwest Ordinance," *Journal of the Illinois State Historical Society* 40:4 (1947), 397.

lakes on a scale unknown in Europe: Dan Egan, *The Life and Death of the Great Lakes* (New York: Norton, 2017), xii.

older than the glaciers . . . ecologically "young": Nancy Langston, *Sustaining Lake Superior* (New Haven: Yale University Press, 2017), 1-3.

one manufacturing belt: Brian Page and Richard Walker, "From Settlement to Fordism: The Agro-Industrial Revolution in the American Midwest," *Economic Geography* 67:4 (1991), 281-315, 283.

Page and Walker: Page and Walker 281-282.

by 1815: Page and Walker 301.

Deborah Popper: "The Middle West: Corn Belt and Industrial Belt United," *Journal of Cultural Geography* 30:1 (2013), 32-54, 33.

Kristin Hoganson: Hoganson 13.

Noble, Vanished Indian: For more on this, see James Joseph Buss, *Winning the West with Words* (Norman, OK: University of Oklahoma Press, 2011).

site of two such attempts: There are so many fun sources about the two Harmonies. My favorites are Marguerite Young, *Angel in the Forest* (New York: Reynal and Hitchcock, 1945) and Martha Bayne, "Utopia Parkway," *The Baffler* 36 (September 2017), https://thebaffler.com/salvos/utopia-parkway-bayne.

poor kid castrated: The most scrupulous historian of Harmony and New Harmony, Karl J.R. Arndt, thinks this is a slander provoked by the jealousy of nearby communities. See Arndt, *George Rapp's Harmony Society 1785-1847* (Philadelphia: University of Pennsylvania Press, 1965), 339.

fails to love humanity: Young, *Angel*, 92.

Mr. Babbitt: Young, *Angel*, 3.

Brooklyn, Illinois: See Sundiata Keita Cha-Jua, *America's First Black Town: Brooklyn, Illinois, 1830-1915* (Urbana, IL: University of Illinois Press, 2002), 1-3.

Arthur Bestor: *Backwoods Utopias* (Philadelphia: University of Pennsylvania Press, 1950), 4.

Marilynne Robinson: See, for example, "Which Way to the City on a Hill," *The New York Review of Books* July 18, 2019, https://www.nybooks.com/articles/2019/07/18/which-way-city-hill/.

reclaim the land: Adam Jortner, *The Gods of Prophetstown* (New York: Oxford University Press, 2011), 13. On the witch-burning part, see 91-100.

are now but one: Jortner 85.

A Shaker visitor: Jortner 86.

acknowledged him: Jortner 90.

bigger even than Cincinnati: Jortner 118.

Black Hawk: Ma-ka-tai-me-she-kia-kiak (Black Hawk), *Autobiography*, https://www.gutenberg.org/files/7097/7097-h/7097-h.htm.

Checagou: The rest of this paragraph relies on William Cronon, *Nature's Metropolis* (New York: Norton, 1991), 23-29.

Writes Emily Lambert: *The Futures* (New York: Basic Books, 2010), 5-6.

Chicago Board of Trade: This description relies on Cronon 111-145.

Norris's language: Frank Norris, *The Pit*, https://www.gutenberg.org/files/4382/4382-h/4382-h.htm.

suppositious villages: Cronon 32.

the way planets cluster: Cronon 39.

You advertise in Omaha: Meridel Le Sueur, *North Star Country* (New York City: Duell, Sloan and Pearce, 1945), 241-242.

Richard White: *Railroaded* (New York: Norton, 2011), 461.

Andreas Malm: "The Origins of Fossil Capital: From Water to Steam in the British Cotton Industry," *Historical Materialism* 21.1 (2013), 15-68, https://geosci.uchicago.edu/~moyer/GEOS24705/Readings/From_water_to_steam.pdf.

earning something was better than earning nothing: Cronon 85-86.

fixed timetables: Cronon 98.

thined out: Cronon 111-116 in particular.

lifeblood of the transcontinentals: White 47.

Matthew Josephson: *The Robber Barons* (San Diego: Harvest, 1934), 84-85.

Nancy Langston: Langston 15.

Plains buffalo: Sierra Dawn Stoneberg Holt has a fascinating counterintuitive take on this environmentalists' commonplace, however: see "Reinterpreting the 1882 Bison Population Collapse," *Rangelands* 40:4 (2012), 106 and following.

Railroads fed demand: See White 461-66.

Kill every buffalo: David D. Smits, "The Frontier Army and the Destruction of the Buffalo," *The Western Historical Quarterly* 25:3 (1994). This quote appears on page 328. Apparently military historians still argue about this, but the paper trail Smits amasses seems conclusive to me.

Granger: See John Collins, "West Coast Grange Wars," *In These Times* June 14, 2015, https://inthesetimes.com/rural-america/entry/18029/a-grange-war-what-goes-around-comes-around-the-west-is-wild.

Charles Francis Adams: "The Granger Movement," *The North American Review* April 1875, 391-424, 396.

opposed black farmers' interests: Dale Baum and Robert A. Calvert, "Texas Patrons of Husbandry," *Agricultural History* 63:4 (1989), 37.

Henry Ford: *My Life and Work* (Garden City: Doubleday, 1923), 3.

Greg Grandin: *Fordlandia* (New York: Picador, 2010), 73.

not really sustainable: *Fordlandia* 69.

Adam Smith: *The Wealth of Nations* Book V, Chapter 1, Part Three, Article II, https://www.marxists.org/reference/archive/smith-adam/works/wealth-of-nations/book05/ch01c-2.htm.

farm and factory life: Grandin, *Fordlandia* 58 (and following for the rest of the section).

Kenneth Kusmar: *A Ghetto Takes Shape* (Champaign, IL: University of Illinois Press, 1978), 12.

Erie Canal: Kusmar 10.

John Brown: Kusmar 3.

"the walking city": Kusmar 34-35.

Turner: See Turner 1.

Gray: "Stories Written in the Blood: Race and Midwestern History," in Cayton and Gray, *The American Midwest* 127.

Frank Harris wrote: Qtd. in Greg Grandin, *The End of the Myth* (New York: Metropolitan Books, 2019), 2.

Van Wyck Brooks: For more on the history of the "revolt against the village," see Jon Lauck, *From Warm Center to Ragged Edge* (Iowa City: University of Iowa Press, 2017).

General Motors strike: For a good popular account of this period, see Edward McClelland, *Nothin' But Blue Skies* (New York: Bloomsbury, 2013), 1-30.

Galbraith: *The New Industrial State* (New York: Houghtin Mifflin, 1967).

businessmen, mechanics: David Graham Hutton, *Midwest at Noon* (Chicago: University of Chicago Press, 1946), xiii.

realistic, matter-of-fact: Hutton 321.

one unpleasant experience: Hutton xiii.

extremes and violent challenges . . . male virtues: Hutton 17.

enterprise, vigor: Hutton 331.

on this favored nation: Hutton 341.

Buley: *The Old Northwest Pioneer Period* Vol. 1 (Bloomington: Indiana University Press, 1950), 12-13.

but meager materials: Caroline Kirkland, *A New Home—Who'll Follow?* http://www.dotwebb.com/regional_writing/new_home/newhome3.html.

Sujey Vega: *Latino Heartland* (New York: NYU Press, 2015), 29.

"bump club": Thomas Sugrue, *The Origins of the Urban Crisis* (Princeton, NJ: Princeton University Press, 1997), 28.

knockout game: See Emma Roller, "The 'Knockout Game' Trend is a Myth," *Slate* November 25, 2013, https://slate.com/news-and-politics/2013/11/why-the-knockout-game-trend-is-a-myth.html.

Ida B. Wells: *The History of the East St. Louis Massacre*, https://digital.lib. niu.edu/islandora/object/niu-gildedage%3A24051.

don't flash back: See Mary Schmich, "This Rumor Relies on Fax, Not Facts," *Chicago Tribune*, September 15, 1993, https://www.chicagotribune. com/news/ct-xpm-1993-09-15-9309150210-story.html.

Vanessa Taylor: "Black and Midwestern," *Catapult*, March 13, 2018, https://catapult.co/stories/ black-midwestern-on-the-mississippi-and-sites-of-memory.

Tanisha C. Ford: "Traveling While Black, *Belt*, June 19, 2019, https:// beltmag.com/traveling-black-indiana/.

Just a few years ago: See Aaron K. Foley, *How to Live in Detroit Without Being a Jackass* (Cleveland: Belt, 2015), *passim*.

Lyz Lenz: *God Land* (Bloomington: Indiana UP, 2019), 6.

ICE: Jessie Higgins, "ICE needs jail space in Midwest, but communities resist," upi.com, August 14, 2018, https://www.upi.com/Top_News/ US/2018/08/14/ICE-needs-jail-space-in-Midwest-but-communities-resist/4871534159291/.

"turned to radiance": Marilynne Robinson, *Gilead* (New York: FSG, 2004), 245.

"wasn't much I could say": *Gilead* 231.

Wendell Berry: "A Native Hill," *The Art of the Commonplace* (Berkeley, CA: Counterpoint, 2002), 25.

Micheaux: *The Conquest* (Lincoln: Bison Books, 1994). Originally published 1913. All quotes 9-10.

Carol Bly: "From the Lost Swede Towns," in *Letters from the Country* (New York, NY: Harper and Row, 1981), 4.

O'Gieblyn: *Interior States* (New York: Anchor Books, 2018), 7.

Thomas Frank: "The Democrats' Davos Ideology Won't Win Back the Midwest," *The Guardian* April 27, 2017, https://www.theguardian.com/commentisfree/2017/apr/27/

democratic-party-2018-races-midwest-populism-trump.

Sarah Smarsh: "Kansas: Aftershocks from the Epicenter of Voter Suppression," *Columbia Journalism Review*, October 4, 2018, https://www.cjr.org/special_report/kansas-midterms-kobach-voter-suppression.php/

Roxane Gay: "Black in Middle America," *Brevity* 53 (2016), https://brevitymag.com/nonfiction/black-in-middle-america/.

Solomon Barkin: "The Decline of the Labor Movement, and What Can Be Done about It," (Santa Barbara: Center for the Study of Democratic Institutions, 1961), 11.

A 1980 *New York Times* story: William K. Stevens, "Detroit and Houston Reflect Shifting Fortunes," *New York Times* July 16, 1980, A12.

David Halberstam: *The Reckoning* (New York: William Morrow, 1986), 58.

financialization: See James Galbraith's introduction to the reissue of his father's *The New Industrial State* (Princeton: Princeton UP, 2007), xvii-xx.

Quality is Our Concern: Barry Bluestone, "Detroit and Deindustrialization," *Dollars and Sense* September/October 2013, dollarsandsense.org/archives/2013/0913bluestone.html.

price risk: See John Lanchester, *IOU* (New York: Simon and Schuster, 2009).

refinery: Ralph E. Wirtz, "Pollution stretches back years," *Midland Daily News*, January 4, 2002, https://www.ourmidland.com/news/article/Pollution-stretches-back-years-7047346.php.

Hoganson: Hoganson 136.

Earl Butz: Tom Philpott, "A reflection on the lasting legacy of 1970s USDA Secretary Earl Butz," *Grist* Feb. 8, 2008, https://grist.org/article/the-butz-stops-here/.

Paul Volcker: See Jeff Spross, "The forgotten recession," *The Week* April 18, 2016, https://theweek.com/articles/618964/forgotten-recession-that-irrevocably-damaged-american-economy.

paying off, at higher rates: "1980s' Midwest farm crisis remains in farmers' psyche," *Minneapolis Star-Tribune*, April 1, 2017, http://www.startribune.com/glut-of-off-lease-vehicles-makes-it-good-time-to-buy-used/417721923/?refresh=true.

Osha Gray Davidson: *Broken Heartland* (Iowa City: University of Iowa Press, 1996), 54.

row-crop agriculture: See, for example, Virginia Gewin, "Farm Runoff in U.S. Waters," *CivilEats*, May 8, 2018, https://civileats.com/2018/05/08/farm-runoff-in-us-waters-has-hit-crisis-levels-are-farmers-ready-to-change/.

Putting antibiotics: Melinda Wenner Moyer, "How Drug-Resistant Bacteria Travel From the Farm to Your Table," *Scientific American* December 1, 2016, https://www.scientificamerican.com/article/how-drug-resistant-bacteria-travel-from-the-farm-to-your-table/.

"most protectionist": Sheldon Richman, "Ronald Reagan: Protectionist," *The Free Market* 6:5 (1988), https://mises.org/library/ronald-reagan-protectionist.

Molinari: Joseph A. McCartin, *Collision Course* (New York: Oxford University Press, 2011), 336-337.

harm workers and enrich elites: See Carlos Salas, Bruce Campbell, and Robert E. Scott, *NAFTA at Seven*, Economic Policy Institute, March 31, 2001, https://www.epi.org/publication/briefingpapers_nafta01_index/.

Chad Broughton: *Boom, Bust, Exodus* (New York: Oxford University Press, 2015), 61-65.

"right here in Galesburg": Broughton, 299.

Obama did not: David Macaray, "Friends Without Benefits," *Huffington Post*, August 9, 2011, https://www.huffpost.com/entry/obama-labor-unions-workers_b_922576?guccounter=1&guce_referrer=aHR0cHM6Ly93d3cuZ29vZ2xlLmNvbS88&guce_referrer_sig=AQAAAKmWtOpyDkbXxNraLDj1roEqFZzKAajkhex_RlQd1K9sWoDXGYZFlT-K9_wpw6lz67fwGqVSPlxrLqP6ucTj6yIkC94t QH4NgEFIqr4Wc36PufRCOZ-oEVYxzJ9RyIcaicIU41PmxsG9HS2I5t2j toXqqlqjWdqSGpRrrTcMMllQ.

Matt Christman: I cannot now find the episode. Perhaps you can. https://www.patreon.com/chapotraphouse/posts.

old idea of the frontier: Greg Grandin, *The End of the Myth* (New York: Metropolitan Books, 2019), 1-5.

Vivos xPoint: See https://www.terravivos.com/secure/vivosxpoint.htm. If you're tempted to buy one, flush your money down a toilet instead.

Survival Condo: See survivalcondo.com.

land grabs: Melia Robinson, "Billionaires are Stockpiling Land …," BusinessInsider.com, June 13, 2017, https://www.businessinsider.com/billionaire-doomsday-preppers-escape-plans-2017-6.

Pittsburgh or the Twin Cities: Matt Tomasino, "Outrun Climate Change," greenhome.com, June 22, 2018, http://www.greenhome.com/blog/outrun-climate-change-best-and-worst-places-to-live.

John Nielsen-Gammon: Aria Bendix, "We Asked 11 Climate Scientists. …," BusinessInsider.com, October 9, 2018, https://www.businessinsider.com/where-to-live-to-avoid-natural-disaster-climatologists-2018-8.

Others suggest, specifically: https://www.theguardian.com/environment/2018/sep/24/climate-change-where-to-move-us-avoid-floods-hurricanes, https://grist.org/cities/spared-by-climate-change-the-10-best-cities-to-ride-out-hot-times, https://www.thinglink.com/scene/863891384979947521?buttonSource=viewLimits.

Detroit does not have to worry about rising sea levels: "Detroit and the Rising Rust Belt's Challenge to the Sunbelt," *Financial Times*, September 12, 2018, https://www.ft.com/content/1b44f9aa-89e7-11e8-affd-da9960227309.

have on our staple crop: Marvin G. Perez, "Warming Planet Could Mean Bigger Corn Crops for U.S.," *Bloomberg*, May 17, 2018, https://www.bloomberg.com/news/articles/2018-05-17/warming-planet-could-mean-bigger-corn-crops-for-american-farmers.

drunk driving: @dril, Twitter, 9:20AM, May 9, 2014, https://twitter.com/dril/status/464802196060917762?lang=en.

smart cars: See, for instance, John Kasich, welcome speech to *The Smartland* Conference, September 19, 2018, https://www.ohiochannel.org/video/governor-john-kasich-2018-midwestern-governors-conference-welcome.

Greg Page: "New Report: Midwest Industries Face Economic Risk from Climate Change," Risky Business, January 23, 2015, https://riskybusiness.org/2015/01/23/risky-business-project-finds-midwest-agriculture-labor-and-manufacturing-industries-face-economic-risk-from-climate-change/.

up to 90 percent: Tom Levitt, "The Giant Corporations Behind Your Burgers and Milk Have a Terrifying Climate Secret," HuffingtonPost.com, October 12, 2018, https://www.huffingtonpost.com/entry/cargill-tyson-food-companies-climate-change_us_5bbf272de4b0b27cf47aed47.

Asian carp: Egan, *The Death and Life of the Great Lakes,* xviii.

Nestlé: Bill Chappell, "Michigan OKs Nestlé Water Extraction," NPR, April 3, 2018, https://www.npr.org/sections/thetwo-way/2018/04/03/599207550/michigan-oks-nestl-water-extraction-despite-over-80k-public-comments-against-it.

Ogallala Aquifer: Laura Parker, "What Happens to the U.S. Midwest When the Water's Gone," *National Geographic* August 2016, https://www.nationalgeographic.com/magazine/2016/08/vanishing-midwest-ogallala-aquifer-drought/.

Popper: See Deborah Popper and Frank J. Popper, "The Great Plains: From Dust to Dust," *Planning* 53 (12): 12-18.

Some of our cities . . . some of our states: See National Climate Assessment, "Midwest Effects," https://nca2014.globalchange.gov/report/regions/midwest.

don't know when to bud: "Specialists: Warm winter leaves fruit trees, plants at risk," Purdue University News Service, February 15, 2012, https://www.purdue.edu/newsroom/general/2012/120215HirstFruit.html

At least two Ph.D. dissertations: Arthur Martin Weimer, *An Economic History of Alma, Michigan*, University of Chicago, Ph.D. dissertation, 1935; and Frederick Judson Soule, *An American Village Community*, Columbia University, Ph.D. dissertation, 1909.

essay that appeared in a small literary journal: Robert Vivian, "Town," *The Least Cricket of Evening* (Lincoln, NE: Bison, 2011). Quotes from 35-38.

"Four Futures": Peter Frase, "Four Futures," *Jacobin* December 13, 2011, https://www.jacobinmag.com/2011/12/four-futures/.

moral equivalent: William James, "The Moral Equivalent of War," https://www.laphamsquarterly.org/states-war/proposing-moral-equivalent-war.

Smarsh: See, for exampl,e "They thought this was Trump country," *The Guardian*, July 26, 2018, https://www.theguardian.com/us-news/2018/jul/26/alexandria-ocasio-cortez-bernie-sanders-kansas-james-thompson.

Night Journey: Theodore Roethke, "Night Journey," *New Yorker* June 8, 1940, https://www.newyorker.com/magazine/1940/06/08/night-journey.

American son-in-law: Email from my dad, who read the book, January 4, 2017.

9 781953 368089